HARD
Bastards

HARD
Bastards

Kate Kray

Pictures by
Don Barrett

Published by Blake Publishing Ltd,
3 Bramber Court, 2 Bramber Road
London W14 9PB, England

First Published in Hardback in 2000

ISBN 185782 329 X

British Library Cataloguing-in-Publication Data:

A catalogue record for this book is available from the British Library.

Designed by GDAdesign

Printed in Great Britain by Creative Print and Design (Wales),
Ebbw Vale, Gwent.

3 5 7 9 10 8 6 4

Papers used by Blake Publishing Limited are natural, recyclable
products made from wood grown in sustainable forests.
The manufacturing processes conform to the environmental
regulations of the country of origin.

NO WANNABES, NO PANTOMIME GANGSTERS, JUST THE 24 HARDEST MEN IN BRITAIN.

DEDICATED TO
'The Lovely Harry'

**IN MEMORY OF THE
HARDEST BASTARD BRITAIN
HAS EVER KNOWN:**

**RONNIE KRAY
1933–1995**

Contents

FOREWORD 17

ROY SHAW
25

JOHN DANIELS
59

JOHNNY ADAIR
33

CORNISH MICK
67

VIC DARK
49

CHARLIE BRONSON
75

HARDB

FREDDIE FOREMAN
85

JOEY PYLE
109

BILL
93

FRASIER TRANTER
117

HARRY H
103

ERROL FRANCIS
125

astards

THE BOWERS
133

FELIX NTUMAZAH
163

GLENN ROSS
143

BOBBY WREN
173

JOHN McGINNIS
155

RONNIE FIELD
181

REGGIE PARKER
189

STELLAKIS STYLIANOU
219

CASS PENNANT
201

JOHNNY FRANKHAM
229

STEVE ARNEIL
211

ALBERT READING
239

CONCLUSION 248

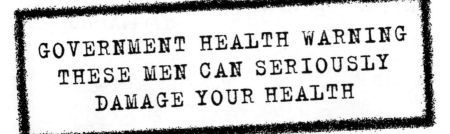

GOVERNMENT HEALTH WARNING
THESE MEN CAN SERIOUSLY
DAMAGE YOUR HEALTH

ACKNOWLEDGEMENTS

I'd like to thank all the hard bastards who contributed and for all their help in tracking down the 'chaps', especially Roy Shaw and Joey Pyle.

Thanks also to Phil Grey of Trade-Sales – if you ever need a new car, Phil's your man; David Ferguson of CPL; Maurice Haskew, assistant photographer; Terry Garwood, computer wizard; Matt Kincade for all his help contacting Johnny Adair; Peter and Sandra from 'Mustang-On'; Linda Calvey; and Lorraine Pyle.

I'm also very grateful to my assistant Lisa Bonnett for all her hard work, and not forgetting Leo. Thanks.

FOREWORD

There are three key ingredients that make a hard bastard, and all tough guys have these three things in common: the three Rs – Respect, Reputation and can have a 'Row'.

DICTIONARY DEFINITIONS
RESPECT – An attitude of deference, admiration, regard, the state of being honoured.

REPUTATION – A high opinion generally held about a person.

ROW – A person who fights and has determination. A battle, struggle, physical combat or punch-up.

The three Rs were the only criteria needed to be included in this book. I interviewed hundreds of men. Some made the grades and some didn't – some I liked and some I didn't. But whether I liked them or not wasn't important. Whether they liked each other or not wasn't important either. The only thing that mattered was that aggression was paramount and part and parcel of their everyday life. They eat it, sleep it and breath it. Violence is their life. This book includes murder, armed robbery and lots of gratuitous violence. I'm not glorifying it or trying to justify the violence, I'm just trying to understand the reasons why some men are prepared to go all the way. If we can understand them perhaps we don't have to fear them.

These men are from right across the board: SAS, murderers, gangsters, terrorists, strongmen and street fighters – you name it, they're all included.

My only rule was that if the tough guy was a bully, there was no way they'd be in my book – full stop. If they were loud, brash or giving it the 'big 'un' – 'I'm gonna do this and I'm gonna do that,' then I left them out. Every man in this book has said, 'I'm not a hard bastard, I'm not a tough guy, I'm not 'orrible – I'm a nice bloke.' I found that more chilling than a man trying to convince me that he's this and he's that.

One man who needs hardly any intoduction is Roy 'Pretty Boy' Shaw. He's a man among men. A 'Bon de Ver' – a man of substance. He's a boxer, a fighter, a walking-talking mean machine. Roy is a self-confessed ruthless bastard and if you're unfortunate enough to have Roy come after you, beware, because hell comes with him!

Take Johnny Adair or 'Mad Dog' – the political

animal, a man alleged to have killed 30 or 40 people. He didn't need to convince me that he was a force to be reckoned with, he just is. I could sense the danger oozing from every pore in his body. I could feel it, almost taste it.

While interviewing Johnny Adair, I can honestly say that anything could have happened. A hired hitman could have had him in his sights or a strategically placed bomb could have had Johnny's name on it. Who knows? There have been ten attempts to kill him and he's only 37. Maybe Lady Luck is looking down on Johnny Adair, or he's got a guardian angel, or perhaps he's too much of a handful for just one man, because if you attack Johnny Adair you'd better hope and pray that you kill him, because if you don't, you'll be the one pushing up daisies.

Big John Daniels. The sheer size of the man, the way he holds himself, his very demeanour is enough to intimidate most people. Everything about him spells violence. His dark shades shield his black, crushed velvet eyes that stare into a secret, hostile world into which no one dares enter. He was the only man hard enough to be trusted with guarding Ronnie Kray's body before the funeral.

Errol Francis is the World Kick-Boxing Champion and Steven Spielberg's minder. He works with all the stars in Britain and America, not only as their bodyguard but also as their personal trainer. He mixes and mingles in the highest of circles. He's a whopping mountain of a man – touch him and he feels like rock.

But Errol has got his feet firmly on the ground. When you meet him, he makes you feel like you're special. He smiles all the time and his laugh is infectious.

Many of the men included in the book dislike each other with a passion. There is one man in particular, whose name I won't mention, shoved a gun up a 'rival's' nose. That rival is also included in the book. After seeing his photograph, the man I was interviewing decided to pull out. I explained to him that he didn't have to like the man or associate himself with him in any way, shape or form. The fact of the matter is that they are both hard bastards and I wanted them both in the book. He is not a fool and rose above his hatred. He shrugged, 'Yeah, fuck him!'

After that I quickly learned to be diplomatic, and careful who I told was included. Each man would sneer and say the same thing, 'I'd do 'im any day – he's not a hard bastard.' So I decided not to show any of them the photographs or to tell them who was in the book. Not because I was bothered about upsetting them, but because I didn't want them to decide to pull out.

Ronnie Kray had a little black address book full to bursting with telephone numbers of all the conmen, murderers and tough guys from all over the country. After we married, I kept a copy of the book in case it was lost or stolen in Broadmoor. I automatically assumed that everybody in the book knew each other, but they didn't, they all knew Ron. He was the king-pin in the middle – the 'Guv'nor'.

Occasionally, I had to telephone these men for

various 'bits of work'. They were villains from as far afield as Wales, Scotland, Ireland and the USA. I got to know them all. Some of them were crazy and unhinged, but they became my friends and, from them, I made more friends. Now I've got a Thomson local directory – the *Who's Who* in the criminal fraternity! The more I got to know them, the more they intrigued me.

I started asking them questions – not about how many people they'd killed or whose body had been buried in which motorway foundations. I wanted to know what made a hard man. What makes a man dangerous? Size? Heart? Love? Money? Passion? Loyalty? Or was it all of these things rolled into one? Is there a link between them? Are there similarities? What makes a man kill? What makes him different? What drives a man to go all the way? Is it in his background? Was he bullied as a child? Is it situation or circumstance? I wanted to interview men who have fire in their bellies and passion in their souls. Those who've got something going on beneath their tough exterior. I wanted to know what makes them tick. Do they have to learn to kill or is it just natural? The questions were endless.

Not all the men I interviewed are from the underworld; there are also law-abiding, straight-up tough guys. Some of the men found it difficult talking about themselves. Some were shy and awkward. But after a couple of visits, they relaxed and started to open up. They'd protected themselves for so long and never let anyone close enough to see them vulnerable or exposed.

Although they were tough men on the street – they can have a row, and can kill – the one thing they were really nervous about was being interviewed and the thing they hated most was the tape recorder. Then it dawned on me that when someone is nicked, the first thing the Old Bill say is, 'You are not obliged to say anything but if you do, it may be taken down and used in evidence against you, blah ... blah ... blah ... ' Every single one of the men was suspicious of the tape recorder. They kept looking at it. It made them uncomfortable and they became 'legal' experts, as if defending themselves. Their voices changed and they started trying to talk in a 'solicitor'-type voice – 'Oh no, I proceeded down the road in an orderly fashion. Those nasty handcuffs are chafing me!' At that point I'd stop the interview, turn the tape recorder off and just get them to relax for a bit.

What's missing from this book, because words don't do them justice, were the men's many gestures. On numerous occasions during our conversations, they'd leap up from their seats and demonstrate with clenched fists exactly how they'd whacked someone, or emphasise the venomous thrust when stabbing a victim. But they never did it to brag or show off; it was simply so that I could get it exactly right. It was then that I saw these men come alive – when they re-enacted their many murderous attacks.

There were two questions that came up time and time again while I was writing *Hard Bastards*. Everybody I spoke to wanted to know which one is the toughest and why? I know who's the toughest. I hope that you can read between the lines and draw your own conclusion as to who is the hardest bastard in Great Britain.

HARD BASTARD

Roy Shaw

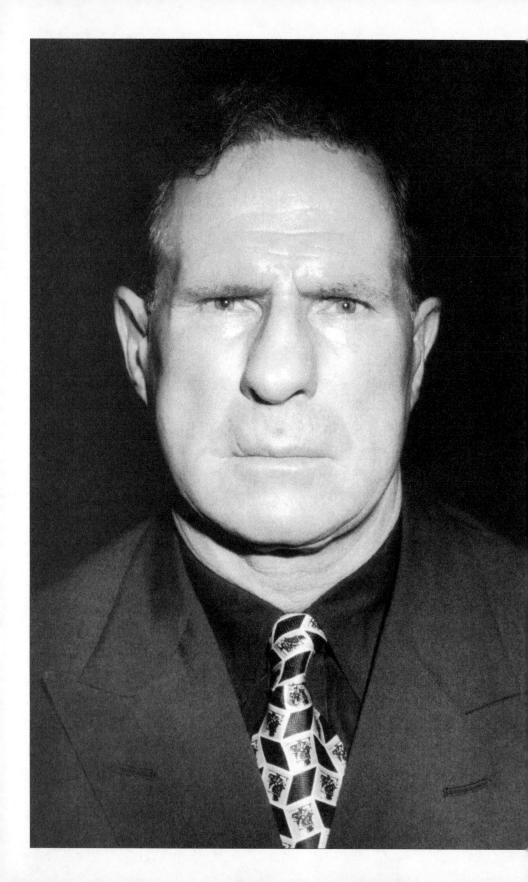

ROY SHAW

Roy Shaw wears designer gear, has a cool million in the bank, a beautiful home and a shiny red Bentley Corniche. He's hasn't got where he is today by being a nice guy. He got there by being the toughest. Everything about Roy spells violence. He is 15 stone of squat, solid muscle, which knots and pops under his silk shirt when he moves. His small, piercing blue eyes are set above a corrugated nose. Roy appears to stare with an unnerving intensity into a secret world of hostility and hatred. In short, he is a walking, talking killing machine.

I met Roy Shaw 11 years ago and in 1999 I was the co-writer of his book *Pretty Boy*. Apart from that, I've got to say that Roy is probably the finest man I have ever met and I've met them all – yardies, gangsters and hard men from all over the country. Indeed, I was married to the most infamous gangster in British history – Ronnie Kray. Ron was the only man who I could truthfully say had the look of the devil in his eyes when he was angry. I didn't think I'd ever see that look again until I met Roy Shaw. Some would say he is Lucifer, Beelzebub, the Prince of Darkness.

But he hasn't got horns sticking out from the top of his head or cloven hooves and a tail; he's just a man, and one with strict principles and morals. Roy has laid down his own boundaries for himself and has never over-stepped the invisible mark or, more importantly, never allowed anyone else to.

Trust is a very hard thing to come by these days, but I would, undoubtedly, trust Roy Shaw with my life. If you are lucky enough to make a friend of Roy, then he is a bloody good friend. Make an enemy of him and beware, because he's a typical male – made up of frogs and snails and puppy dogs' tails. When he's good, he's very, very good and when he's bad, he's horrid.

NAME: Roy Shaw.

DATE OF BIRTH: You're as old as the woman you feel!

STAR SIGN: Pisces.

OCCUPATION: Villain/Gangster/Entrepreneur/Businessman/Nice guy!

BACKGROUND

I was born in Stepney, east London, within the sound of Bow Bells. I'm a true cockney, a Londoner through and through. I was a street urchin, a ragamuffin. I grew up in the war years when times were hard. Our family didn't have much in the way of money but we had plenty of love.

At the tender age of ten I discovered the gift that God had given me – the power of punch. From then on, I became a rascal, getting myself into all sorts of trouble. I was a man on a mission with nothing to lose and a lot to prove.

I became a professional boxer, training under the guidance of Mickey Duff. I had ten professional fights with ten wins, six of them knock-outs.

LIFE OF CRIME

I've been in and out of prison nearly all my life for various different reasons; a little bit of this, a little bit that, 'comme ci, comme ça' – but mainly for crimes of violence. I've spent approximately 24 years behind bars.

WEAPONRY

I'd use my fists, but if someone was armed then I'd also be armed and I'll kill them.

TOUGHEST MOMENT

I was ten years old. I was lying in bed when I heard Mum scream. My elder sisters looked after me while Mum went to the hospital. When she came back her face was ashen.

She sat me down on the sofa, her eyes were red and puffy.

'Daddy's dead,' she whispered.

There had been a terrible accident. A lorry had swerved out of control and one of the pedals of my father's motorbike hit the kerb. Dad tried to regain control of his bike but it was no good, he hit a lamp-post head-on and was killed instantly. That was a long time ago, but I remember it as if it was yesterday and I'm not ashamed to say that it still brings a tear to my eye.

IS THERE ANYONE YOU ADMIRE?

No.

DO YOU BELIEVE IN HANGING?

Yes, I most definitely do, for paedophiles, rapists and perverts.

A man that commits crimes against women and children is not a man, he's a fucking dog and deserves to die like one.

IS PRISON A DETERRENT?

No. I was a hard-working kid before I was put away then I got to know all the 'toughies'. Going off the straight and narrow is nothing new – it's a well-trod path, a natural progression. Borstal, prison, then Broadmoor. I wasn't the first to be put away and I certainly won't be the last, just the handsomest!

WHAT WOULD HAVE DETERRED YOU FROM A LIFE OF CRIME?

Nothing.

WHAT MAKES A TOUGH GUY?

When a child is born it has no concept of skin colour, religion or prejudice. It has to learn how to walk, talk, hate and fight. I think you've got to learn how to be a tough guy. It took a long time and lots of hard graft for me to become as nasty as I am.

ROY'S FINAL THOUGHT

In 1999, I wrote my autobiography *Pretty Boy*. It was at number one in the bestsellers list for more than eight weeks and there is talk of my life story being made into a feature film. I'm not embarrassed to say that I'm as proud as punch, if not a little surprised.

Since writing my book, I've had literally hundreds of letters from kids all over the country, and some from as far away as Australia, saying that my story has given them hope and inspiration. That's the best compliment I've ever received. If I can help prevent one youngster from being bullied, then writing the book was well worth the effort. As a young boy I was bullied; it affected me badly.

My father died when I was ten years old. After that sad day, something inside me died – I just snapped. I wouldn't allow the bullies to bash me any more. Almost overnight I turned from a meek, mild boy into, some would say, a ruthless bastard. If I'm truthful I'd agree and say that, yes, I am a ruthless man. But I didn't set out to get a reputation, that was never my intention. It just happened.

I've hurt, killed, and done some wicked acts of violence throughout my life, but only if a man deserved it. I can honestly put my hand on my heart and say that I have never hurt any women or children. So, I have no regrets or the need to unburden myself and ask anyone for forgiveness. If I hurt ya – fuck ya – you deserved it.

I don't live in the past, because if you live in the past you die a bit each day. I have no pity or conscience and have been called the devil; maybe I am, but when I die I know that God will shake my hand and welcome me into heaven with open arms because basically I'm a nice, ruthless bastard.

HARD BASTARD

Johnny Adair

JOHNNY ADAIR

'I'm not a gangster. I'm not a fighter. I'm a soldier of war.' Spine-chilling words from Johnny Adair, the Unionist.

I'd heard about Johnny through the prison grapevine. Often, his name would crop up in conversation, but I'd never actually met him. In September 1999, I saw a small article in the *Sun* newspaper. There was a photograph of Johnny Adair being released from the Maze prison under the Good Friday Peace Treaty. He was the 293rd prisoner to be released and, as he walked, or should I say strutted, from the Maze, he looked every bit as dangerous as I'd heard he was.

I decided to include Johnny in *Hard Bastards* because he fitted the criteria: he demands respect and has a fearsome reputation, but mainly he can have a 'row'.

It's one thing to decide to put someone in a book, but

then I've got to find them and convince them to take part.

I certainly didn't want to put word out on the street that I was looking for Johnny, or indeed that anyone was looking for him. I know from experience that dangerous men are extremely paranoid.

Usually, if I want to contact a villain I make a call or two and I'll have the number in my hand within hours, but Northern Ireland is not my manor. However, it was amazingly simple to find Johnny Adair. I rang Directory Enquiries and asked for numbers of political parties in Belfast. The operator gave me five or six different organisations and I started to make my calls. I explained each time that I was a journalist and wanted to speak to a man called Johnny Adair.

Instinctively, I felt that what I was doing was not 'politically correct', but I needed to find Johnny. There was a wall of silence. Every answer was the same, a curt, 'You won't find him here. You won't find him there.'

Then I struck lucky. A lady I spoke to shiftily gave me a number and then hung up. I telephoned the number and asked to speak to Johnny Adair. A man with a strong, gruff Irish accent answered, 'What do you want him for?'

I explained who I was and that I was writing a book. The voice on the line became softer, no longer hostile.

He introduced himself as Matt Kincade and said that he had read a couple of my books while serving time in the Maze prison and that Johnny Adair was a friend of his.

The whole exercise had been like looking for a needle in a haystack, and hopefully I'd found it! Within days, Johnny was in touch, but was reluctant to commit to any firm meeting. It was all very cloak and dagger. I told him I would travel to Ireland on 11 November. He gave me a telephone number and told me to ring it when I arrived. With that tiny snippet of information, I booked my ticket on the early-morning flight from Luton to Belfast.

My Easyjet flight to Northern Ireland was delayed – damn, I didn't want to be late. I was going to meet Johnny Adair, or 'Mad Dog' as he is known. I sat on the plane waiting for take-off. I was fed up, it was the one interview I didn't want to miss.

My friends and family had warned me not to go. They all said the same; that I was getting in too deep. I'd heard wild stories about Johnny Adair kidnapping Catholics and chopping them up. Each story was more bizarre than the last. I didn't take any notice; to me it was all just hearsay.

Then I heard it from a good, reliable source that I really shouldn't go; it was too dangerous and I was getting out of my depth.

Being the flippant fool that I am I just replied that I wasn't Catholic or Protestant, but in actual fact I was Salvation Army. I'm a sunbeam, so as far as I was concerned, I was quite safe – or as safe as I could be.

We landed in Belfast on a cold, grey November morning. I made my way to the Stormont Hotel by cab. I was apprehensive, unsure what I was walking into. Maybe everyone had been right after all, and I was putting my life in danger needlessly. My minder stayed close to me the whole time and the photographer said nothing through fear.

When we reached the hotel, we ordered coffee in the lounge area and I rummaged in my briefcase for the small scrap of paper with the telephone number that Johnny Adair had given me. A deep Irish voice was waiting for my call. My instructions were to wait; Johnny would ring my mobile phone at 10.00am sharp. On the button, my phone rang – it was Johnny.

From the start, he was paranoid. He thought it was a set-up and said that if I wanted to speak to him then I was to go to the Shankhill Road.

I said no; I was a girl, I'd come to his back yard, and it was only right that he came to the Stormont Hotel to see me. He laughed, 'I'll be there in half-an-hour.'

I waited outside the hotel for Johnny to arrive. I'm used to dealing with paranoid men and I wanted to put Johnny at ease and, more than anything, to show him that it wasn't a set-up and his life wasn't in any danger. I told the photographer to wait inside and my minder to stay close.

Half-an-hour later I noticed a car circle the hotel. I watched it drive round once, and then again, before pulling up in front of me. Driving the car was a huge man. Sitting next to him was Johnny Adair. He climbed from the car, his eyes scanning everywhere. His minder did the same, his hand inside his jacket. Johnny walked towards me, his greeting warm and sincere. I introduced him to my minder, and he introduced me to his. Johnny's accent was so deep that I had difficulty understanding him.

'This is Winker,' he said, pointing to his minder.

'Sorry?' I answered, with a puzzled look.

'Winker ... this is Winker.'

I shook his minder's hand and said, 'Nice to meet you, Wanker!'

For a moment there was a deathly silence. My minder looked away in horror. Winker's face could have curdled milk. Johnny Adair roared with laughter and from that moment on the ice was broken.

In the beginning, the Irishman wanted to do the interview in the back of a car while it drove around the city streets of Belfast, but I convinced Johnny to go inside the hotel.

As we walked through the car park, a police car drove past. Johnny stopped dead in his tracks and glared at the patrol car. The officers inside looked at Johnny. I saw the panic in their eyes. Johnny stared daggers at them. They looked away. Johnny shot a glance at his minder and they both smiled.

We settled in the hotel foyer and ordered our coffees. I sat with Johnny on a sofa while our minders and the photographer sat some distance away.

Before he agreed to be in the book, Johnny wanted to know what it was all about. I explained about the book and showed him some of the other photos of a couple of men who were already included. In a strong Ian Paisley accent he said, 'I'm not a gangster. I'm not a fighter. I'm a soldier of war – a fucking terrorist!'

The entire time I was in Johnny's company, I felt that at any moment something could happen. I didn't quite know what, but it was extremely dangerous being in his presence. His eyes flickered around the room all the time, scanning and surveying, watching everybody's move – as did his bodyguard.

We started to talk and he became a little more relaxed until somebody sat behind me. His piercing blue eyes widened with alarm. He motioned to Winker. Suddenly they were on alert.

'Do you know the man sitting behind you?' he whispered.

I glanced over my shoulder and shook my head. It was obvious that Johnny was now uncomfortable. He never took his eyes off the man and Winker stayed close. He may have thought the man was from the security forces, the IRA or just a hitman who'd come to kill him.

It all seemed a little far-fetched until Johnny took his hat off and showed me the hole in the back of his head, the size of a 50p piece. Two months earlier, he'd been shot in the back of the head at a UB40 concert.

Then he lifted his sweater and showed me a hole in his side and one in his leg. He had been almost cut in half in another attack and there has been over ten attempts to kill him.

As Johnny talked and his story slowly unravelled, it was a tale not about money, or a grudge – Johnny Adair was fighting for what he truly believed in, which was for peace in Northern Ireland. I told him it was difficult for me to understand, because all we are used to seeing on the mainland are the atrocities that are committed in Ireland.

Before going to Northern Ireland, I didn't have any preconceived ideas about Johnny Adair. But I didn't expect him to be as 'normal', or as warm and friendly as he was. Everyone expects terrorists to be gun-toting thugs, but that's not the case. Johnny spoke with great intellect. There was no malice or bitterness in his voice. It was the cool, controlled way in which he spoke that made him so utterly terrifying. He was normal – just like you and me. Before I went to Northern Ireland, I really hadn't known what to expect, but I wasn't prepared for the Johnny Adair that I met.

At the end of the interview Johnny agreed to have a photograph taken outside Stormont Castle, where the peace talks were taking place. We left the hotel and stood on the kerb, waiting to cross the busy main road. There were four lanes full of traffic. Every car in the four lanes stopped to let Johnny cross because they had recognised him. It was unbelievable. This is the power he has in Ireland.

Johnny was very amicable until the photographer asked him to turn his head and look at the castle. He refused. Johnny still wasn't sure if it was a set-up. After the photo shoot, Johnny Adair was whisked away by his minder as quickly as he'd arrived. This is his interview.

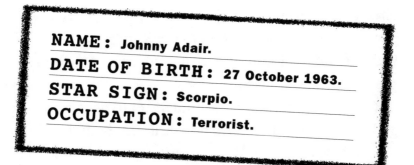

NAME: Johnny Adair.

DATE OF BIRTH: 27 October 1963.

STAR SIGN: Scorpio.

OCCUPATION: Terrorist.

BACKGROUND

I was born in the Shankhill Road area of Belfast, Northern Ireland. I'm the youngest of five brothers and one sister. As a teenager, I ran with a gang of Protestants. We'd roam the city centre searching for Catholics to hurt, for no other reason than their religion.

To people on the mainland, this may sound extreme but unless you live in Northern Ireland, the constant troubles are difficult to understand. I can only describe Belfast as two nations – Protestant and Catholic – and, believe me, the two don't mix. It can be likened to the combination of nitroglycerine and a detonator – separately they are safe, but put them together and it's dynamite! The wars were bloody and there were many casualties on both sides. I bear many scars and war wounds from my endless street battles. I think my reputation came from being a paramilitary leader, even before I was involved in the politics of it.

I was a young Loyalist, full of hate and anger, and saw Catholics as my enemy. I was a product of the Troubles in Northern Ireland. I grew up on the streets. Fighting Catholics was all I knew. I was a loose cannon, with no direction, until, that is, I joined the paramilitaries which gave me the direction I needed. It was then I realised why I was fighting: for peace in my country. Freedom is a passion I truly believe in.

It's every human being's fundamental right to be free and I'd fight until the last breath in my body to achieve this independence. I became ruthless in my quest and would stop at nothing. It was then I earned respect and got my reputation.

LIFE OF CRIME

I've been in and out of jail all my life, all for terrorist offences. In 1995, I was charged with 'Directive Terrorism' and was sentenced to 16 years. Directive Terrorism covers a lot of things but I can't for legal and security reasons talk specifically about what I have done. In September 1999, I was the 293rd prisoner to be released early under the Good Friday peace deal.

WEAPONRY

Again, for legal and security reasons I cannot say what I specialise in.

TOUGHEST MOMENT

I've had many tough moments. There have been ten attempts on my life. I've been attacked with crowbars and hammers and stabbed twice, in the back and in the leg. I've been shot and wounded three times, once by the IRA. They ambushed my car and opened fire with an assault rifle. I was hit in the side of my body. But the worst pain I've ever experienced in my life was being shot at close range in the back of the head. It was the most petrifying moment I've ever had.

It was Autumn 1999 and I'd just been released from Ulster's top-security Maze prison on parole. I'd promised to take my wife to a UB40 concert. We'd been looking forward to our first night out in many years. The kids were safely tucked up in bed and the babysitter was due at any time. As we were getting ready, there was nothing to suggest that this night was ever going to be anything out of the ordinary.

The atmosphere at the concert was electrifying. UB40's rhythm was contagious. My wife and I swayed to the dulcet tones, 'Red, red wine ...' It was good to feel normal again, if only for a moment.

BANG! The panic, the fear, the confusion. My wife screamed. I slumped to the floor with a bullet lodged in the back of my head.

IS THERE ANYONE YOU ADMIRE?

There are people I admire in Ireland who, in my eyes, are heroes. For instance, Michael Stone, the lone sniper in a Catholic graveyard. It's difficult for me to explain and I certainly don't mean any disrespect to London gangsters, but there are things terrorists would do in two days that gangsters wouldn't do in their lifetime. That's just a symptom of what's happening in Northern Ireland. Atrocities aren't being committed on a personal level, it's aimed at the enemy and we believe the things we are doing are part of defending our people. If this means going to the extreme, then so be it.

DO YOU BELIEVE IN HANGING?
No.

IS PRISON A DETERRENT?
In Ireland, prison is not thought of as a deterrent, although a few years ago things were different and prison

would have been harder but not these days. In Ireland, the paramilitary run the prisons, not the screws. We're not criminals, we're paramilitaries; we're classed as soldiers. When we go to jail, we don't do what they tell us – they do what we tell them.

Jail is not a deterrent, jail is an education. I learned more about life when I was in jail than I did in the whole of my lifetime when I was out.

In jail, you're confined 24 hours a day and that time is spent alone. Outside time just passes you by and you never have time to stop and think about anything. Inside, you're on your own, you analyse everything, you have all the time in the world to think, so it's an education because everything goes through your head about what happened in the past, what might happen in the future. You analyse it all and educate yourself – it's self-education. The fact that you're in jail can be used to your advantage – if you want exams, you learn; if you're into training, you use your time in the gym. That's what I did. I went into jail out of shape and came out in the best shape of my life.

No, jail is not a deterrent, it's an education. The only thing it does is take away your freedom.

WHAT WOULD HAVE DETERRED YOU FROM A LIFE OF CRIME?

Nothing would have deterred me because I fight for what I believe in, and when you believe in something you follow your heart.

I strongly believe what I've done is right so I have

followed my heart. The only thing that will stop me from fighting is peace in my country.

WHAT MAKES A TOUGH GUY?

Only one man in a thousand is really tough. It's natural – just in them. It's not something you can share or explain, it's just in you and people notice it and feel it.

IS THERE ANYTHING TONY BLAIR COULD DO TO HELP PEACE?

I think Tony Blair has done all in his power and I praise him for that. He has taken risks to please everybody. He has released hundreds of prisoners, both Loyalists and Republicans, so I believe he genuinely wants peace in Northern Ireland. I don't think there is a lot more he can do. He has given it his best shot. From day one his support has been second to none, so I praise him, I really do.

JOHNNY'S FINAL THOUGHT

I have no regrets in my life except that so many people have lost their lives. It's just a shame that peace didn't happen in Northern Ireland 30 years ago. The peace that we have now and the talks that are presently taking place should have happened in 1969. Then there wouldn't be over 3,000 people dead today, both Protestant and Catholic. That's the only regret I have in the role that I played.

In September 1999, I was released from the Maze prison. I'd served five years of a sixteen-year sentence.

Now I'm mellowing back into the community. Things have changed since I've been away – for the better. At last there is peace, but not for me.

When I was inside, I let my guard down. When I came out of prison I thought I was safe to go to a UB40 concert with my wife – I was wrong.

Now I don't go anywhere without a minder. I have to live in a house that is protected like a fortress; all steel doors and security cameras. I have men sitting at the bottom of my street day and night to watch me and my family. Every day I wake up expecting something to happen and not knowing if it's going to be my last day on earth.

The only thing that gave me a wee bit of breathing space was the Shared Government, but look what happened to that.

I don't fear for myself, I fear for my family. I believe that it's me with the death sentence hanging over my head. If I thought any different, I would have been up and away years ago.

First and foremost, I have no fear of the IRA or anyone else. If I did, I would be living in England. But I'm not, I'm still living in Belfast. I live 50 yards from a peace line that proves I have no fear of them.

The security forces nicknamed me Johnny 'Mad Dog' Adair. In their eyes, I'd killed over 40 people. They built up this myth that I was a Mad Dog who would kill anyone. People expect me to be a fanatical, violent, rabid dog. It's not the case – I'm Johnny, and deep down inside I'm a good guy. But, do me a wrong and I'll bring it to your own back yard. You'll go to bed at night and barricade your front door in case Johnny 'Mad Dog' Adair comes looking for you.

HARD BASTARD

Vic Dark

VIC DARK

'I played for high stakes and lost. The judge sentenced me to 48 years in prison.

'Standing in the dock were the "cozzers"; they smiled and shook hands, the no-good slags! Next morning I woke up in one of Her Majesty's Prisons and there I stayed, in a world full of terrorists, crazies and murderers. There is precious little left to truly shock the bejesus out of me, except betrayal by a friend – or a so-called friend!'

I was sitting in a flash office in Tottenham, east London, interviewing Vic Dark – some call him 'The Man'. The office looked like it belonged to JR Ewing from the popular soap *Dallas* – all heavy oak panels and comfortable leather chairs. It was Vic's brother's office, the owner of a successful company. A condition of Vic's parole is that he has a job, so his brother employed him!

'It pissed the screws off when, on my release from

prison, my brother picked me up in his brand-spanking-new Bentley convertible,' Vic sniggered.

Vic's mood soon changes when he mentions a former friend who I'll call 'Jock'. He curses and snarls with anger cat having spent 12 years inside for him. Vic continues, 'I should have shot the slag. Put one in his nut ...'

It is a story beyond belief. Vic spoke with such venom and anger, as if it all happened yesterday. The wounds were so obviously still raw.

Vic and 'Jock' were on an armed robbery. There was a bit of a hiccup and Vic shot a security guard. To be precise, he blew his fucking thumb off! Some hiccup! 'Jock' panicked and called Vic's name, then rushed to help the guard. Vic shot the guard again; the bullet went through the guard and into 'Jock'. They were supposed to be professional armed robbers but it was quickly turning into a farce. Alarm bells rang, sirens wailed and police surrounded the building.

Vic had to decide whether to leave 'Jock' behind or take him with him. Vic's eyes bulged through the slits in his balaclava as if he'd taken an ounce of 'whizz'. But he had no need for illegal substances – he was high on adrenalin.

Vic decided to help his friend and pulled his balaclava off. He was hot and sweaty and it felt good to feel the cool air. He picked up his wounded mate and carried him out of the building, armed to the teeth, screaming at police, 'Stand Back or I'll shoot.'

He took a policeman hostage and put his mate in the back of the police car. He aimed his gun at the terrified officer's head, then made him drive. The officer was rigid with fear as the car sped off into the distance.

In the ensuing chase, somehow the gun went off, the bullet whizzing past the officer's head. The officer wanted to be invisible. He tried desperately to sink ever deeper into the driver's seat. Sweat poured from his forehead. He put his hand up to guard his head, pleading for his life, 'Don't kill me, please don't kill me.'

Vic wasn't going to kill him. At the time, his mind was racing. A million scenarios went through his head. Killing the Old Bill was the last thing on his mind. The car took off, hell for leather, through the streets of London until they reached leafy suburbia.

The car screeched to a halt outside a secluded house in the middle of nowhere.

Vic made the officer carry his wounded friend towards the house where he proceeded to kick the door in, much to the surprise of an Irishman called John Stackpoole, who was quietly eating his dinner. There was none of the usual Irish blarney like 'Top of the morning!' or 'Wattleygetcha?' It was more a case of, 'WHAT THE FUCK ...?' Vic wasted no words and demanded the keys to the stunned Irishman's car. After bundling his wounded mate and the officer into the motor, he had no choice but to take the Irishman hostage as well.

My jaw dropped open. I gasped, I couldn't believe what Vic was telling me. Vic shook his head.

'I know, I know, the whole story sounds fucking unbelievable. But it's true, every single word, and it gets worse ...'

As the car sped away at high speed, armed response units were called and a high-speed chase, accompanied by helicopters, snaked its way across London. It was complete mayhem. The next port of call was a Chinese restaurant, but not for a take-away – Vic needed a new set of wheels. After several shouts and threats, another hostage joined the not-so-merry day-trippers, a man called Lam Quang Tran.

The whole thing was gathering speed and momentum like a runaway train. They all had a one-way ticket to nowhere – a fucking nightmare! Vic had to get away. He had to dump all this excess baggage.

Finally, it all came to a shuddering halt. But not in a station, in a fucking potato field of all things. Vic dumped the hostages and had it away on his toes. He was fully loaded with all guns blazing, the Old Bill in hot pursuit. He made his way to the middle of the field and buried himself under the mud and spuds, with both arms by his sides holding a gun in each hand. He waited and waited. Police with snarling dogs combed their way through the field looking for the desperado. Vic never moved a muscle. At one point, an officer stood on Vic's leg; still he waited. For eight hours he lay in the muddy potato field. But it was a waiting game which Vic inevitably lost.

Vic stood in the dock and was sentenced to 48 years behind bars. 48 fucking years for a so-called friend. Vic seethed, 'I should have put one in his nut and saved myself a lot of heartache ...'

NAME: Vic Dark.

DATE OF BIRTH: 12 April 1957.

STAR SIGN: Aries.

OCCUPATION: Ex-armed robber

BACKGROUND

I'm an EastEnder, from Forest Gate, Stratford. My dad's Maltese and my mum's English. I've got one brother. I left school and went into engineering, but it wasn't for me.

I met a girl from a place called Wanstead and she took me to her house – it was absolutely beautiful. It was at that point I noticed rich from poor. From that moment on, I decided I didn't want to end up like my dad, working every day that God sends and still ending up saving only £1 a week in the Post Office. That's not knocking my father, it's just not how I wanted to live.

I was always into combat sports: karate, kick-boxing, a little bit of this and a little bit of that. Then I found out about a thing called a gun and away I went.

I started off robbing building societies when I was 17. It was quick and easy money and I loved it.

LIFE OF CRIME

I was 20 years old when I was first put on remand, for stabbing. All my offences have been for shooting and firearms. I've been acquitted for two attempted murders.

When I go to prison I don't get a day off for parole. I go in category A and come out category A. I do not concede to the prison system. I've just completed a 12-year sentence.

WEAPONRY
I've been convicted of stabbing and shooting. Who dares wins!

TOUGHEST MOMENT
My toughest moment was being sentenced to 48 years for helping a so-called friend. I took the rap for taking three hostages, whilst on an armed robbery. My so-called mate had been shot. I could have put a bullet through his head and walked away, but I didn't.

The hardest point was going on a visit and explaining to my family why I gave up my life for a friend. They couldn't understand it. In retrospect, neither can I.

IS THERE ANYONE YOU ADMIRE?
Anyone with good principles. Men of the old school, like Joey Pyle. He's a man of his word.

DO YOU BELIEVE IN HANGING?
No. Hanging is a terrible way to die. While I was in prison, I found six people hanging in their cells. One inmate, a man called Jimmy Collywood who'd served 14 years, was in the cell opposite mine and he hanged himself. In the morning I found him. For a time, it affected me badly. The image of Jimmy hanging in his cell, with his tongue hanging out and his eyes bulging,

stayed with me for a long time. It's something I'll never forget.

Another reason why I don't believe in capital punishment is if an innocent man is hanged. It's no good granting them a pardon if they're dead. There are many innocent men serving life imprisonment for crimes they haven't committed. One that springs to mind is a bloke called Warren Slaney, he's serving life and he is innocent. I've nothing to gain by lying. It's the truth.

IS PRISON A DETERRENT?

No, prison is not a deterrent. When a man commits a crime, especially the act of murder, he doesn't worry about going to prison, he doesn't even think about it.

WHAT WOULD HAVE DETERRED YOU FROM A LIFE OF CRIME?

Money; if I was born in to a wealthy family. I never want to take second best. I've been chasing money since I was 17 and I probably always will.

WHAT MAKES A TOUGH GUY?

To get respect, you've got to be nice. If you're a dog, no one likes you. I don't class myself as a nasty person and I don't attack people for nothing, but if you go through the penal system and come through it unscathed, you've got to be fairly tough. It's all right being tough on the streets, but if you've got 30 screws outside your cell all with riot shields and batons and you're not frightened to steam into them, that sorts the men from the boys.

VIC'S FINAL THOUGHT

I'm not a nasty person. Believe it or not I've got a conscience; if I was having a row, I would stop if it went too far but only if I knew I'd won. But if I thought I was going to get a kicking, then I'd take you out of the game. No question. That's one of the reasons why I gave up the guns. If I'm gonna die, I'll take a lot of people with me.

HARD BASTARD

John
Daniels

JOHN DANJELS

'Kinda broad at the shoulders and narrow at the hip. And everybody knows you don't give no lip to Big John...'

That's a line from a song that springs to mind every time I see John Daniels. The man is a mountain, an immovable object. He's 6ft4ins and weighs 30 stone. He looks every bit what he is – Big Bad John.

The first time I saw John Daniels was in March 1995. The reason that date is so prominent in my mind is because it was the day I buried my husband Ronnie Kray. John was the man assigned to guard Ronnie's body in the Chapel of Rest at Bethnal Green, east London. At the time, I didn't get to speak to John or even acknowledge him; in actual fact, I never saw him again until the day I saw a photograph of him in Nigel Benn's autobiography *Dark Destroyer*.

Through a friend of a friend, I found out his name and managed to track him down to Luton, Bedfordshire. I telephoned him and explained about the book. John was softly spoken, he wasn't loud, brash or aggressive. He didn't try to be something he wasn't; he didn't have to. John is what he appears to be – a hard bastard.

John agreed to meet me and talk, at a pub in Shooters Hill in South London. I've done quite a few interviews at this particular place but each time I've felt a strange atmosphere there. On this particular day, it was worse. Out of politeness, I asked the lady serving if I could take some photographs in the bar. There was no moment of consideration, just a flat 'No'. I didn't feel that was a problem, it was her pub and she could do what the hell she liked. John eventually had his photographs taken in a subway in South London.

When we returned to the pub to do the interview, I switched on my tape recorder and we started to talk. Almost immediately, music blared from a sound system. It was The Commitments blasting out their version of 'Mustang Sally'. The noise was deafening; we could barely hear ourselves speak. At first, we ignored the loud music. This just irritated the landlady and she turned it up to full volume. We battled on against all odds to do the interview.

Once we'd finished, I thanked John for having driven such a long way and taking part, but also apologised for the way we had been treated. I thought the landlady had made a fool of me – mugged me off – so, before I left, I felt I just had to have a word in her ear.

Leaning nonchalantly on the bar was a middle-aged, peroxide-blonde woman reading a newspaper, a fag hanging from the corner of her mouth. I asked if I could speak to the landlady. Without looking up from her paper, she spat, 'You're speaking to her.'

Small droplets of saliva cascaded on to the bar. Her very demeanour aggravated me. I asked what the problem was and why had she turned the music up so loud?

'I wanna know what you've been talking about,' she snarled.

I told her it was none of her goddamn business.

'Oh yes it is, it's my pub,' she continued.

I was incensed, absolutely livid. How dare she? What's it got to do with her what we were talking about? I was just about to get out of my pram when at that moment John came over and explained he was about to leave. I saw the landlady lift her eyes, which instantly widened.

She looked towards heaven as if she was looking at a skyscraper; the ash fell from her cigarette. John couldn't have chosen a better moment to walk over.

The argument was starting to heat up; John's sheer presence defused the situation. He gave me a hug and a kiss and said goodbye.

I turned to continue the conversation with the landlady but she'd lost the sting from her tail, she wasn't sassy any more. I should imagine John has this effect wherever he goes, but he's a bit of an enigma. Nobody knows much about John, which reminds me of another line of that famous song.

'Nobody knew where John called home. He just drifted

into town and stayed all alone. He didn't say much he's kinda quiet and shy. And if you spoke at all you just Hi To Big John … Big John … Big Bad John …'

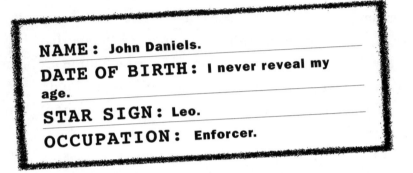

NAME: John Daniels.

DATE OF BIRTH: I never reveal my age.

STAR SIGN: Leo.

OCCUPATION: Enforcer.

BACKGROUND

I've got three brothers and a sister; I'm the middle son. I didn't get into many fights at school because of my size. I've always been big, naturally big. At 13 years old I weighed 16 stone. If I did get into a fight at school, it was generally with older boys.

From leaving school I started minding small clubs and I suppose it was from then on my reputation grew. Nowadays, I spend most of my time as a celebrity bodyguard, both in London and Brooklyn, New York.

LIFE OF CRIME

All the time I've served inside has been for violence; debt-collecting that went over the top or an over-zealous fan of the star I'm minding. I never go out looking for trouble – trouble is my work. It's just part and parcel.

WEAPONRY
My hands. My fists. That's all the weapons I need.

TOUGHEST MOMENT
When my father died. I've known lots of hard men but my father was the hardest I've ever known. Not just because he was my father, he was one tough cookie.

IS THERE ANYONE YOU ADMIRE?
My dad Joseph, he died eight years ago.

DO YOU BELIEVE IN HANGING?
That's not just a 'yes' or 'no' answer. I personally do not agree with the death penalty. Having said that, I'm a father and if anyone abused my children I'd kill the perpetrator stone dead. It doesn't make it right but that's what I'd do. An eye for an eye. But capital punishment is cold-blooded murder and that's wrong – it's a civilised society killing someone for killing.

IS PRISON A DETERRENT?
No. Track record proves it. Look how many prisoners are repeat offenders.

WHAT WOULD HAVE DETERRED YOU FROM A LIFE OF CRIME?
To be honest, I don't think anything would have deterred me. Most people in my world would be in it no matter what. It's partly circumstances and also the make-up of that person.

WHAT MAKES A TOUGH GUY?

A man who doesn't use violence for violence's sake. Like when you see a bouncer on a door, a big guy, who has a reputation to match, then a 5ft drunken office worker abuses him. The doorman stays cool, he knows he can take him out at any time but he doesn't, instead he tells him to run along and saves it for another day. If he was to take advantage of the situation and bash the office worker, that would make the big guy a bully, not a tough guy. How I see it, if someone is drunk and can barely stand, there's no glory in bashing him up. I don't have anything to prove. Little dogs bark, big dogs bite!

BIG JOHN'S FINAL THOUGHT

I've had more than my fair share of fights but I evaluate every situation. There have been circumstances where I've been outnumbered three to one; it's then I make my judgement. Are they going to go away without a fight? If I come to the conclusion they're not, then I'll lash out first. I usually come out on top. I would fight to the death if I had to, it doesn't matter how outnumbered I am, I will go forward. I've never gone down. My father always said to me, 'If you're going forward when you go down, then you've won …'

HARD BASTARD

Cornish Mick

CORNISH MICK

Normally, when a man reaches a certain age or when his beer-gut swells, he seeks out a personal trainer. But not Cornish Mick. In his younger, thinner days, he used to do a bit of boxing. He's from the school of hard knocks and is a little bit 'tasty'. Mick tenderly pats his beer belly and winks, then he holds up his right index finger and smiles. 'That's all I need. It takes one finger to pull a trigger.'

Mick can't be bothered with all the puffing and panting, sweat and toil from training down the gym. He's not a man who'll waste words or make idle threats – no matter how big a man is, he just lets his finger do the talking.

He's a cutter; a shooter; a killer. Upset him and he'll pop a cap in your arse and bury you in the woods sooner than look at you. I know – I have first-hand experience of Mick's bad temper.

It was late Saturday night. Yet another gangster do. Men in hand-made dinner suits. Villains' wives, all lipstick, powder and paint. I sat at the top table with the top men all smoking the best Cuban 'Lah-di-dahs'.

Mick sat beside me. We chatted and laughed about this and that, until a big man in a cheap suit started making a bit of a nuisance of himself. He was a wannabe gangster, a loud-mouth with nothing to say and saying it too loud.

I remember thinking with a foolish sense of annoyance that I wished the geezer would just go away. Mick's eyes narrowed. There was no mistaking he was beginning to get irritable.

Mick no longer listened to what I was saying. His mind was elsewhere. The loud-mouthed, plastic gangster was getting on his nerves.

Mick stood up, shrugged his shoulders and straightened his tie. His eyes looked spiteful. I had never seen Mick like this before. He walked over to the geezer and told him to fuck off. Mick said it with conviction. Then he said it with some scorn. His voice grew more determined, more positive. The loud-mouth spluttered and stammered, 'Err ... Err ...'

Suddenly from his back pocket Mick pulled a blade. The loud-mouth was no longer loud; with no more words, no more warnings, Mick dragged the blade slowly down the man's cheek.

His eyes widened to the size of saucers as he clutched

his face. Blood, the colour of fine red Chianti, trickled through his fingers. Mick pulled a crisp white handkerchief from the top pocket of his bespoke suit and handed it to the man. Then he coolly hailed a cab. He helped the man into the taxi with as much concern as a scorned woman. Mick turned to me, 'Sorry, Kate, where was we?'

NAME: Cornish Mick.

DATE OF BIRTH: 10 February 1935.

STAR SIGN: Aquarius.

OCCUPATION: Gangster.

BACKGROUND

I was born in Cornwall. There's nothing much to say about Cornwall except that the pasties are nice! The eldest son of two brothers and two sisters. My dad was in the Army most of the time, so the discipline was left to my mother, and I must say she was a dab hand with a broom handle!

I came to London when I was 42 years old, after I'd been round the world doing various naughty things. I followed my heart, and a girl, to London. The romance didn't last long. When I got some 'bird' she pissed off with someone else. Aah well, you can't win 'em all. But I stayed in London – on business of course!

LIFE OF CRIME

I've been away for 18 years altogether but have been sentenced to about 35, most of which were for crimes of violence and armed robbery.

WEAPONRY

I only need one finger to beat the biggest man in the world – my trigger finger.

TOUGHEST MOMENT

Losing my dad, I think, was the toughest moment in my life. He died in 1963 when I was in Dartmoor. The screw unlocked my cell and told me straight that my dad had died. I couldn't even get a day out for the funeral.

IS THERE ANYONE YOU ADMIRE?

Joey Pyle. He's a fair man, he's loyal, he'll stick to his guns and he won't turn anyone over. What you see is what you get with Joe.

DO YOU BELIEVE IN HANGING?

For crimes against women and children – yes, I do.

IS PRISON A DETERRENT?

While you're young it's not, the consequences just go over your head. You don't think about getting caught or else you wouldn't do the crime. Every thief in the country believes he will never get caught – someone else, but never him.

I know some of the hardest men around who cry

themselves to sleep because they just cannot stand being locked up. Then there's people like Reggie Kray and Ronnie Fields. They don't do it easy, they do it the best way they can. When you get to a certain age, you look back and think about everything you've missed and start to think twice. I'm 65 now. I don't want any more bird.

WHAT MAKES A TOUGH GUY?

Pride is a part of it. If you've got pride in yourself, there's no way you'll be made a mug of. It's not muscular development or anything like that. I know little blokes that are as hard as nails. I think it's pride and having a sense of right and wrong. If somebody does you wrong, then you've got to do something about it. It's hard to put into words. You can have a bloke as big as a house that can't hold his hands up because he just hasn't got the heart. Having a heart plays a big part in being a tough guy.

MICK'S FINAL THOUGHT

I don't feel in danger in my local pub just having a quiet drink. But there are times when I go out and stand with my back to the bar and watch certain people all night. To me, Roy Shaw was one of those. Although he's straight with his mates, if I didn't know him I'd be very, very careful. I think it's the unpredictability of some people's nature. Ronnie Kray would fly into a rage for no apparent reason, like swearing in front of a lady. Roy Shaw is exactly the same. Something would snap in Roy if he thought you were taking the piss. You can say what you like to me, but if you take the piss or if I thought my life was in danger or I was going to get nicked, I'd kill you – no hesitation.

HARD BASTARD

Charlie Bronson

CHARLJE BRONSON

I visited Charlie Bronson – the most dangerous prisoner in the penal system – at Woodhill Prison, Milton Keynes. Woodhill is a top security prison and has a specially designed unit for men with no release date and nothing to lose. It's a prison within a prison, known as Britain's Alcatraz.

Charlie has spent 22 years out of the last 26 in solitary confinement in prisons like Woodhill. He has been locked in dungeons, in iron boxes concreted into the middle of cells and, famously, in a cage like the fictional Hannibal Lecter. He has endured more periods of isolation than any other living British prisoner, spending months at a time with nothing more than cockroaches for company. He is always held under maximum security, in a spartan cell with little more than a fire-proof bed and a table and chair made from compressed cardboard. When he's unlocked, up to 12 prison officers – sometimes in riot gear and with dogs – are standing by.

I arrived for my visit half-an-hour early. I parked my car and went to the reception desk, told them my name and gave them my passport for identification.

I wasn't told to sit with other prison visitors but was shown into a small, secure room. An officer handed me a piece of paper with a number on and motioned his head towards a large tray. I was then told to remove my jacket, shoes and watch ready to be searched. I passed through an X-ray machine identical to the ones you find at airports. I was then asked to move to another area and stand on a special box with both my arms out in order to be searched.

I was asked to open my mouth and lift my tongue. An officer looked in my ears and up my nose, then felt under my arms, around my chest and down my body. I had to lift my feet so that they could examine in between my toes. I was then told to lean back and throw my hair forward. I asked what they were looking for – concealed drugs and weapons. Eventually, I was given back the tray containing my possessions and permission was granted for me to continue to the next gate accompanied by three officers.

'Lima two six, lima two six, permission to walk?' whispered one of the officers into a small radio. Each step of the way was the same; at each gate, permission had to be granted before we could move on. I was led into the final reception area where I was thoroughly searched for the second time.

The only thing I was allowed to take into the inner sanctums of the prison was a bag of loose change for the vending machines. Charlie had left a list for me; he wanted six chocolate bars and four bottles of Buxton spring water. I had awful trouble with the vending machines, it was taking such a long time. An officer came in and said that Charlie was getting agitated and they would sort his shopping list out for me later.

I continued my journey through the prison; surveillance cameras followed my every move. I was spooked by the eerie silence. Two huge male officers opened a small room containing two long tables. One table had one chair on one side and three chairs on the other. Sitting at the other table were four officers.

They stood up as Charlie was brought in. He was wearing a chequered pea-green and canary yellow boiler suit. He had a shaven head and a beard down to his naval – oh, and little round sunglasses like John Lennon used to wear. Charlie smiled; so did I. A puzzled look came across his face and he asked in a gruff voice, 'Are they your real teef?'

I put on my best smile and replied, 'Yeah.'

Charlie walked towards me, and suddenly the officers were on alert,

'Can I tap 'em?' he asked.

I exposed all my pearly gates for him to tap. Gently with his finger, he proceeded to tap my teeth one by one.

'Ooh lovely,' he cooed. 'Sit down, let's have a chat.'

We settled down in the small, cramped room. Six officers, Charlie Bronson and me. This is what he said.

NAME: Charlie Bronson.

DATE OF BIRTH: 6 December 1951.

STAR SIGN: Sagittarius.

OCCUPATION: Hostage-taker, serving life imprisonment.

BACKGROUND

I have two brothers – John and Mark. My childhood was like any other – 'mad'!

LIFE OF CRIME

I've been in prison for 26 years. I'm still Category A. I hold the record for the longest-serving prisoner in solitary confinement – 22 years. I'm currently kept in a cage naked and fed through a cat flap.

WEAPONRY

My most dangerous weapon is my madness and unpredictability. I have a problem where I just change in a spin and become something that's not human. I'm not really a wicked man but put an axe in my hand and I'll show you an abattoir.

TOUGHEST MOMENT

Holding a guy by his feet from a balcony 18 floors up and deciding whether to let go. I pulled him in. I regret it because the man's a rat. Maybe next time!

IS THERE ANYONE YOU ADMIRE?

My medicine ball – Bertha.

DO YOU BELIEVE IN HANGING?

Yes, all paedophiles should hang. There is no cure for them. Kids are innocent and scum who kill them should be hung.

IS PRISON A DETERRENT?

No, prison is not a deterrent. How can it be? Prison breeds tougher villains.

WHAT WOULD HAVE DETERRED YOU FROM A LIFE OF CRIME?

Love, understanding and apple pies!

WHAT MAKES A TOUGH GUY?

Feelings and fairness. A man's got to have them, or he's not a man. Without feelings you're a mutant.

CHARLIE'S FINAL THOUGHT

I was in Broadmoor for the criminally insane in a dormitory and Gordon Robinson was in the next bed. He was bugging me. I'd hit the fucking idiot once before, but I knew our paths would cross again, and there he was in the next bed.

My mother and father had just been to see me. I was feeling happy. After the visit I went back to the ward and found Robinson with his key in my locker. The toe-rag was trying to open it. A locker thief! Prison rule by cons, number one – do not steal from other cons. I pushed him away, then I chinned him. But that wasn't enough for me. I wanted to kill him, he deserved to die. He was going to die.

I've got a silver tie that my dad had given me some years ago. My favourite tie. I locked myself in the toilet and tested its strength on the toilet cistern. To my surprise, it held my weight. I decided to strangle Gordon Robinson that very night. I was excited. It was the same buzz I got from doing armed robberies. I walked into the dormitory in my pyjamas with the tie round my waist, out of sight. I climbed into bed and waited.

Robinson's left eye was almost closed from where I punched him earlier. His other eye was alert. I smiled my best smile.

The night patrol nurse looked in every half-an-hour through the observation slit in the door. I only needed a couple of minutes. Fuck the night watchman! There was no saving the thief. I lay still, deep in thought, the tie wrapped around my wrist under the blankets, just waiting. Like a spider waits for the fly. Time was plentiful, I had all night long. This was my night, my fly – I was buzzing. Twelve o'clock, one o'clock, I waited patiently watching every bed, watching every movement. Then it happened, as if I'd sent the thief a telepathic message. He moved. He sat up. He bent over to put his slippers on. He was probably going for a piss.

I leapt out of bed. In a second, the tie was wrapped around his ugly neck. I was strangling the locker thief. It felt magic, it felt right. Surprisingly, there was very little noise – a sigh, a groan at first, but then nothing. I pulled tighter, and leant over to watch. His eyes bulged, his face went grey, his tongue protruded. Dribble ran from the corner of his mouth. He pissed himself, I smelt shit. He was on his way out of planet earth. Then it happened, the tie snapped. I had half the tie in one hand and half in the other. He began making noises, loud animal grunts, deep chesty moans. Other patients began to stir. Now I was in trouble. I acted fast. I punched him in the face and straddled over his bed. I shouted to the loons that he was having a nightmare but the purple welts around his neck told their story.

The next four years I spent in Broadmoor's hell-hole – the punishment blocks – and I never got the opportunity to strangle Gordon Robinson again!

HARD BASTARD

Freddie Foreman

FREDDJE FOREMAN

Freddie Foreman resembles the sinister character of Mr. Christie from the notorious horror film _10 Rillington Place_. He's softly spoken. His eyes stare unblinkingly. He's a man who has done what he's done and doesn't give a fuck who knows it!

One of the things that I didn't know was that it was Freddie Foreman who was with Reggie Kray when Ronnie died, on St Patrick's Day in 1995. Freddie was in Maidstone prison when he was told that Ron had died. When he heard the news of Ronnie's untimely death he asked to be taken on to Reggie's wing to comfort him. As soon as Reggie saw Fred, he burst into tears and hugged him. Fred comforted Reg the best he could.

They had a long friendship that stretched over more than 40 years. A jug of green hooch appeared from another friend and Fred stayed with Reg all day. They talked of the old days and of fond memories of Ron. The inmates kept them supplied with more jugs of green stuff.

They weren't hungry, but sandwiches came by the platefuls – tuna, ham and more green stuff. The old friends stayed together for a day and a night. Reg asked Fred to be a pallbearer at Ronnie's funeral.

When Fred told me this story some five years later while I was interviewing him for this book, his voice cracked with emotion. I saw Freddie Foreman with a tear in his eye as he remembered his old friend. Who says that tough men don't cry?

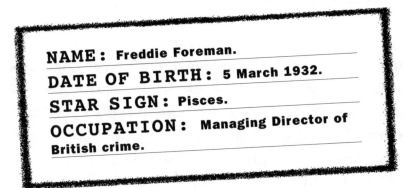

NAME: Freddie Foreman.

DATE OF BIRTH: 5 March 1932.

STAR SIGN: Pisces.

OCCUPATION: Managing Director of British crime.

BACKGROUND

I am one of five brothers – Wally, Herbie, George and Bert. All of us are products of the war years. Unlike my brothers, I was too young to serve in the Army, so I lived off my wits and thieved off the pavement. By the time I was 18, I'd become a full-time thief. My social life was exciting and fulfilling and I was fit and ready to take on the world.

LIFE OF CRIME

I've been sentenced to 20 years in prison for murder and disposing of a body, but have served 14 years.

WEAPONRY

I was a professional boxer and had over 40 professional fights. So I would say that I can have a 'straightener', but I prefer to use a gun.

TOUGHEST MOMENT

On my birthday, I was sentenced to ten years for disposing of Jack 'The Hat' McVitie's body. I was taken to the cells beneath the court and was given another ten years for murdering Frank 'the Mad Axeman' Mitchell. I'd say that was a tough moment and a pretty shit birthday!

IS THERE ANYONE YOU ADMIRE?

Ed Bunker, who served 20 years behind bars in America. He played Mr Blue in the film *Reservoir Dogs*. Once released from prison, he didn't just blend into the background, he got on with his life and became a successful writer, writing magnificent books like *Runaway Train* and *Dog Eat Dog*.

DO YOU BELIEVE IN HANGING?

No, definitely not. It's been proven that innocent men have gone to the gallows. Perverts and child abusers should not be hanged, they should be chopped up and fed to the dogs. Myself, I would like to take them fishing.

IS PRISON A DETERRENT?

No. Prison is a breeding ground for crime, but what else is there? Short, sharp, shock treatment was a good idea. National Service was a good idea; tagging another. I think the answer today is to educate kids. Ninety per cent of tearaways can't read or write.

Once the hormones start kicking in, we have a problem. Testosterone is a powerful thing. If we shake up our education system and revise the National Curriculum, then perhaps things will change.

WHAT WOULD HAVE DETERRED YOU FROM A LIFE OF CRIME?

A good education. It would have been easier to earn money the straight way rather than the crooked – less hazardous.

WHAT MAKES A TOUGH GUY?

Tough guys are a rare breed. But when you come across a real tough man, you've no doubt. They are courteous, polite, not loud and full of veiled threats. You sense their danger; almost taste it. A smiling viper!

FREDDIE'S FINAL THOUGHT

Old professional criminals don't exist any more – Maggie Thatcher took care of that. She gave the police a licence to shoot armed criminals in certain circumstances. While she was in government, more armed robbers were shot dead than at any other time. Modern technology has taken care of the rest – surveillance cameras are everywhere.

Nowadays, most crime is drug-related. Petty crimes by petty criminals. Drugs frazzle brains, leaving the person with no morals or standards. I'm one of the old school where there was honour amongst thieves. When I was at it, I wouldn't have dreamed of burgling a neighbour's house. It was the 'haves and have-nots'. I'd target big banks, post offices and security companies. I'd never hurt the normal man in the street; I'd only hurt other gangsters if they did me a wrong or crossed me in my line of business.

Sure, I've gunned down quite a few men throughout my life – Frank Mitchell and Ginger Marks, to name but two – but I don't regret murdering them one bit. After killing them, I wrapped them up in chicken wire attached to weights and buried them far out at sea, away from fishing lanes, deep beneath the cold, muddy waters of the English Channel. I'd been told by an American friend that bodies weighed down in this way would never find their way to the surface but would slowly be devoured by crabs and other deep-sea creatures.

There has always been great speculation and mystery surrounding the demise of Jack The Hat, Frank Mitchell and Ginger Marks, and how their bodies were disposed of. Only a few people – perhaps a handful of close friends – knew that it was me that took them on a fishing trip!

The only regret I've got in my life is that I'd like to have killed a couple more men, but, lucky for them and unfortunately for me, I missed 'em! Oh yeah, and the other regret I've got is being caught. Must dash, I'm going fishing.

HARD BASTARD

Bill

BILL

Bill's hair is short and spiky, a chaotic mix of styles that blends into one hip hairdo.

'I ask myself,' he says, plopping down into a leather Chesterfield armchair in his jeweller's shop in east London, 'what the fuck am I doing here? Why do you wanna interview me? I ain't no hard bastard.'

I smiled a nervous smile. 'I beg to differ, Bill.'

How can a man that looks like Bill say he's not a hard bastard? If ever a man's face told a story, then Bill's is a novel. He's blacker than black and meaner than mean. His combat boots and trousers scream, 'VIOLENCE, VIOLENCE, VIOLENCE.' His fists are like club hammers; his stubby arms are built like well-oiled machine tools, ever pumping and grinding. The impression that Bill leaves is that if you were stupid enough to hit him over the head with a bottle, it would have about as much effect as the champagne magnum that launched the QEII. His voice booms with authority. When he says, 'sit', not only the dog in the room sits, so does everybody else. Let's face it, if you saw Bill in a dark alley walking his dog, would you be comfortable walking past him, or would your heart pound that little bit faster? Let's say it how it is – Bill is one mean mother-fucker. No ifs, buts or maybes.

Life is full of surprises. It wasn't until half-way through our interview that it dawned on Bill my name was Kray. To our amazement, I discovered that years ago Bill used to visit Ron in Broadmoor. An unlikely visitor you might ask yourself? Ron liked people for who they were and not for the colour of their skin. Racial prejudice was at the top of his list of pet hates.

I met many people while I was married to Ron, all of whom played some part in the murky depths of the underworld – murderers, bank robbers and villains of all shapes and sizes including 'yardies'. If they'd been to visit Ron, they would have been up to 'no good' and involved in some kind of 'naughty business'. Put it this way – they certainly wouldn't have been 'straight-up geezers'.

Once Bill and I had established that he'd been a friend of Ron's, he became more relaxed and opened up. He spoke warmly of Ron and, from the way he spoke and the things he said, I knew that he had at one time been a good friend to Ron. It's a small world.

I'd never met or heard of Bill but he'd been recommended to me for the book by the 'highest authority'. He had come with the glowing reference of being one of Britain's hardest bastards. As the interview progressed, I slowly peeled away the hard coating that Bill had built up over the years to protect himself. There was layer upon layer of animosity and anger. As we stripped away the protective shell, there were times Bill had difficulty in expressing himself. The top and bottom of it is that he's just a violent, angry young man – full stop.

Bill smiled – a rare smile. For a moment, his face changed. It was no longer hostile, as if someone had turned a light on in his eyes.

'Well, Kate, if you say I'm a hard bastard, then I guess I am!'

NAME: Bill.

DATE OF BIRTH: 15 December 1961.

STAR SIGN: Sagittarius.

OCCUPATION: I do a lot of minding work for the stars – Wesley Snipes, a lot of the rap stars and also some rich Arab people who carry a lot of money around with them.

BACKGROUND

I was brought up in Whitechapel, east London. Then my family moved to south London. I've got two brothers and two sisters. I'm the eldest boy. I was bit of a nuisance at school but nothing out of the ordinary. My parents were fairly strict. I had a good upbringing but I wasn't over-privileged or anything like that. I suppose from day one I was getting myself into problems, but I was just mischievous. Although Mum didn't see it like that; she was always up the school for one thing or another.

To keep me off the streets, more than anything, I started training and body-building – not for competition reasons, just for the sake of keeping fit.

I had a period when I didn't keep fit and I went up to 28 stone, had a 64in waist and I could hardly walk or breathe. I didn't like that feeling and have never stopped training since. I'm fitter and more agile at my present weight of 23 stone.

LIFE OF CRIME

I've been to prison once and that was enough for me. I've done lots of bad things and never been caught for them. Ironically, I did time for a relatively minor offence. A policeman was taking pictures of me and all I did was take the film out of his camera!

When I got banged up, I thought to myself, this ain't me, this is not a clever place to be, and no matter what it takes, I never intend doing any more 'bird'.

WEAPONRY

I can never tell what situation I'm gonna be in. I like to use my fists if I have to, but I will always try to avoid violence. Unfortunately, I've got a bit of a temper, so anything could happen. I'm not frightened to use tools and have done in the past, but it depends whether it warrants it or not. I never commit violence unnecessarily. I'm not one of these guys who'll use my position to bully people.

In my view, bullies always come unstuck. My motto in life is, 'The man who's frightened is the man you've got to be careful of!' He knows he's got to take you out of the game, because if he doesn't, he knows he will die. Simple!

TOUGHEST MOMENT

When I went to New Orleans, I had a little confrontation with the Ku Klux Klan. I was on holiday with my girlfriend, and we were having a wonderful time. We went to the Grand Cayman Islands, then to Disney World, and we ended up in New Orleans for the Mardi Gras.

While thumbing through some brochures in the hotel lobby, we saw an advert for an Island Swamp Tour. My fascination with alligators got the better of me and spontaneously we booked two tickets for the following day.

The sun was hot as we waited to board the small boat to take us into the swamp. With an outstretched hand, a Ranger snatched our tickets, and as he did I noticed tattooed on his hand the letters KKK – Ku Klux Klan. The Ranger didn't acknowledge me, in fact he didn't even look in my direction. He just turned his back and started speaking into a small radio.

'We got a nigger on board the boat...'

By now I was getting bad vibes. But I thought, fuck it, I've paid my money to see the alligators, I'm just gonna go. At that moment, I didn't realise just what danger I was in. I looked around the boat and there was a sea of white faces – it was only then it dawned on me how serious the situation was.

As we set off through the swamp, the Ranger went through the motions of 'the helpful tour guide' and passed snapshots around the boat. When he got to me, for the first time we had eye contact. 'Pass it over, boy,' he hissed.

The Ranger could see I was no mug and I wouldn't back down. He didn't argue, in fact he never said a word. He just turned the boat round and headed back to shore.

As I stepped off the boat, there were 12 armed Sheriffs waiting for me. I was in trouble – big fucking trouble. I wasn't in London, I was in New Orleans, America's deep south, where black men are lynched. All of them wanted a slice of my black ass. I'm not ashamed to say, but I was scared. Man, was I scared.

'Hey, boy,' one of the officers asked in a slow American drawl, 'are you that nigger on the telly, Mr T?'

My mind was racing and my heart pounded.

'Er … er … yeah, that's right, I'm Mr T …'

For the first time in my life, I was happy to be mistaken for this character.

The mood changed. He actually asked me for an autograph for his kids. Then he warned me, 'I trust you won't be round these parts again. People go missing round here, BOY.'

I got my black ass out of there as quick as possible because there was no doubt they were definitely gonna have some fun with me.

IS THERE ANYONE YOU ADMIRE?

God.

DO YOU BELIEVE IN HANGING?

I do believe in hanging for perverts, but saying that, there can be no mistakes.

IS PRISON A DETERRENT?

To the majority, I don't think it is a deterrent. In fact, if you go to jail, you become more knowledgeable about crime. You're associating with criminals, so what do you expect? To some people, one bit of 'bird' is more than enough. In my case, I felt like a caged animal. I'm not saying that if I had to go to prison I wouldn't be able to do the 'bird', because I know I can. It's just something I'd rather avoid.

WHAT WOULD HAVE DETERRED YOU FROM A LIFE OF CRIME?

Nothing would have deterred me. It's not something I planned to do, it just happened. If I need money or whatever, I'll do what I have to do. It's just survival.

WHAT MAKES A TOUGH GUY?

A man who tries to avoid violence and doesn't use unnecessary force. I believe in warning people first. If that doesn't work, I say, 'In the name of God, man, think carefully, you don't fucking want this!' I always quote God's name. But there's always one who wants to push it.

Respect – if a man hasn't got that, he's got fuck all.

Then I have no choice, I take him out.

BILL'S FINAL THOUGHT

Racism has come a long way. There is still institutionalised racism, but that will always be there; you've got to accept that. People will always have their views, no matter what.

If people make comments about my colour, the way I react depends on the situation; whether I'm with my girlfriend, my kids or whether it's worth the fucking bother.

Sometimes I have to wipe my mouth; I think it's harder for a man to wipe his mouth than to kill someone. Taking someone's life isn't an easy thing to live with, I don't care how hard you think you are. That's the worst regret I've got. They've got families, it's not just you it affects. It leaves a trail of shit behind. Murder – it's a messy business!

HARD BASTARD

Harry H

HARRY H

Harry is 'quintessentially English'. The 'Lovely Harry', as his mates call him, is as English as black cabs, double-decker buses and red telephone boxes. He wears finely tailored Savile Row suits and Fratelli Rossetti crocodile shoes. He carries an ivory cane and has perfect double cuffs which he adjusts at regular intervals. He is today's David Niven or Trevor Howard.

Harry possesses a taste for the good life and a sense of mischief that no true English gent is complete without. Whether it's driving around in Jaguars and Rollers or eating 'speed' like it's going out of fashion, he takes his pleasures wherever he can. He sails through life without leaving a shambles behind; behaving reasonably well, being honest, a man of his word and, not least, having a good time.

But Harry was born with a streak of mischief running through him. He's not your average nine-to-five man, never has been and never will be. He likes to think of himself as an entrepreneur who will, on impulse, try anything once.

Nowadays, he tells me that he's given up the 'dirty rat race'. But like the true English gentleman that he is, he's retired to a quintessential cottage in the country, with quintessential roses around the door, a quintessentially wire-haired fox terrier by his side, and an all-singing, all-dancing, waving, African grey parrot called Claude who Harry has taught to stutter.

Harry adjusts his cuffs and straightens his tie for the last time during our interview. He lovingly hands Claude a monkey nut while trying to convince me that he's retired and is now a virtual recluse. Claude interrupts with a squawk and a screech, 'He's a g-g-g-good boy now!'

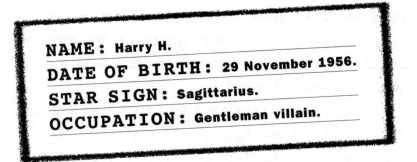

NAME: Harry H.
DATE OF BIRTH: 29 November 1956.
STAR SIGN: Sagittarius.
OCCUPATION: Gentleman villain.

BACKGROUND

I was born and brought up in the garden of England – Kent. I have an older brother and an older sister. I was a normal kid from a normal family. I looked up to my father; he was a good man. My mother was the disciplinarian; she tried her best, bless her heart. I've always been a loner, I find it better that way. If I don't trust anyone then I won't be let down. I think it was my destiny to be a rascal. Even from the age of 13, I was heading down the wrong road, when I was busted for drugs.

LIFE OF CRIME
Nothing to speak of – only drugs, firearms and fraud!

WEAPONRY
When I was younger, I was hot-headed and would have a tear-up with anyone. Now I'm older, I realise there is more than one way to skin a cat!

TOUGHEST MOMENT
Realising my 13-year marriage had fallen apart.

IS THERE ANYONE YOU ADMIRE?
Great leaders, like Churchill. He was a strong man, a leader of his time.

DO YOU BELIEVE IN HANGING?
No. If we are to believe to take someone's life is evil, then it's evil across the board. Society is wrong to take a life. They are as guilty as the person they are trying.

IS PRISON A DETERRENT?
Like a lot of things, prison is only a deterrent until you've experienced it. It's fear of the unknown.

WHAT WOULD HAVE DETERRED YOU FROM A LIFE OF CRIME?

A family.

WHAT MAKES A TOUGH GUY?

To me, a tough guy is a man who believes in something enough to kill or be killed. Great men like Malcolm X, the Irishman Michael Collins and the Scot William Wallis. They all died for a cause they truly believed in.

HARRY'S FINAL THOUGHT

The first thing a man should take into consideration before embarking on a life of crime is his family and his loved ones. Also, honour, pride, self-respect and his word are all important. A man is nothing if he's not true to his word. It's not easy to take another man's life. I know from experience you'll never be the same person, no matter who you are. Everyone has a conscience, whatever way he disguises it with excuses.

In his heart he knows not only that the person has died but there is an innocent party left behind, hurting.

HARD BASTARD

Joey Pyle

JOEY PYLE

Joey Pyle is the archetypal gangster, like the Godfather, Don Corleone. He wouldn't look out of place in movies like _The Long Good Friday_ or _Goodfellas_. Joey has ruled the roost in the underworld for more than four decades. He is the original 'Teflon Don' – nothing sticks.

Each and every man I interviewed for this book had either known or heard of Joey Pyle. He is the most respected of them all. I've never heard anyone say a bad word about him; whether that's through fear or admiration, I'm really not sure. Either way, he's held in the highest esteem by everyone.

The beauty of Joey Pyle is that he has the capability of mixing in any circles, whether it be royalty, celebrities, MPs or murderers. He's at ease with them all. Maybe it's this quality that has given him longevity in the underworld. He is a man of few words, a shrewd businessman, someone you'd be reluctant to approach without an introduction. His very size and presence is enough to make you take a step back.

His hair is black, slicked back with grey around the sides, making him appear very distinguished. Remove his dark sunglasses and they reveal twinkling blue eyes that are soft around women and cold as ice to men.

He has the ability to hold everyone at arm's length and you're only in Joey's company if you're invited. No problem is too big for Joe and he can minimalise any problem with just a word or wave of his hand. Wherever he goes he is well respected, but only a fool would take his kindness as a weakness.

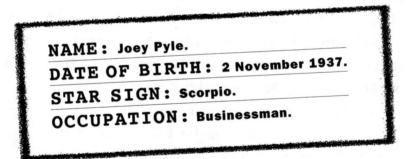

NAME: Joey Pyle.

DATE OF BIRTH: 2 November 1937.

STAR SIGN: Scorpio.

OCCUPATION: Businessman.

BACKGROUND

I was bought up in Islington, the eldest of four children. The greatest influence in my life was my dad's twin brother, Joe. He was the ABA and Amateur Welterweight champion of Great Britain. As a child I used to watch him box and loved every minute of it. Inevitably, I followed in his footsteps and started boxing at 12 years old at the Angel in Islington. Boxing came easy to me and I was bloody good it at it as well. I won loads of trophies, eventually becoming the schoolboy boxing champion of Surrey. I'd won all there was to win as an amateur so therefore turned professional. I had 22 fights as a professional boxer. I lost my first and last fight to a boxer named Maxie Beach. It was at that moment I decided to become a gangster instead of a fighter.

LIFE OF CRIME

I have always been a bit of a rascal. In 1955 when I was 18 I did my first 'screwer' [burglary]. It was a TA hall and I was stunned when I walked away with seven grand in my pocket. Seven fucking grand, what a result!

It was the easiest money I've ever earned. This gave me the taste for hard cash and started me on the road to a life of crime. I've never looked back since. Over the following years I thieved 'on the pavement', which is the polite way of describing pillage and plunder. It got me into all sorts of trouble.

In all, I've been arrested 50 times and have been sentenced to 35 years in prison. I've spent 15 years behind bars. I've been tried at the Old Bailey, Court Number One four times: for robbery, drug smuggling and murder. But each time I've been found 'not guilty', of course.

WEAPONRY

My brain is my biggest weapon.

TOUGHEST MOMENT

The hardest battle was seeing my mother die in September 1999. Her death knocked me for six, as if something inside me fell on its side.

IS THERE ANYONE YOU ADMIRE

Joe Louis, nicknamed 'The Brown Bomber' – the greatest boxer that ever lived.

DO YOU BELIEVE IN HANGING?

No. If one innocent person is hung, then the system is wrong.

IS PRISON A DETERRENT?

No – but what else is there? Prison is not meant as a deterrent, prison is meant as a punishment.

WHAT WOULD HAVE DETERRED YOU FROM A LIFE OF CRIME?

Nothing or no one would have deterred me.

WHAT MAKES A TOUGH GUY?

It's not the size of a man, nor his stature, but his heart and his principles. A man could be 4ft tall, but if he is a man of his word he gains respect from those around him. Only then he becomes a tough guy.

JOEY'S FINAL THOUGHT?

I've no remorse, no conscience and no regrets for the things I've done in my life. The one thing I've always believed is that a still tongue keeps a wise head. If you gamble with the Devil, the Devil will win.

HARD BASTARD

Frasier Tranter

FRASJER TRANTER

Frasier Tranter is a big bloke. In fact he's gigantic in size, height, weight and power. Fortunately, as I'm in the iron grip of his huge handshake, I realise I'm standing slightly down a slope from him and he is in fact only 6ft 10in, and not the 9ft that it seems.

I'd waited four months to interview Frasier. Each time I phoned him to ask when he was in London, it was always the same answer:

'My wife is pregnant. I don't want to leave her.'

Most 35-year-old blokes with film star looks are concentrating on getting pissed and pulling the lycra-clad blonde dancing round her handbag in Stringfellows. But not Frasier; he's an amiable and down-to-earth bloke who likes nothing more than spending time with his family in Wolverhampton and training – that is, when he's not taking calls on the telephone, something he did a lot throughout our interview. Frasier bristled with pride and smiled one of those new father smiles.

'My wife gave birth to a baby boy. I've got a son. I'm a dad.'

Mention tough guys and his face changes dramatically.

'I don't like gangsters,' he sneers.

Whoops! I was unsure if he knew that I was a Kray. If he didn't like gangsters then he was talking to the wrong person. Tentatively, I asked him if he knew who I'd been married to.

'Oh, yeah, the Krays. They're different …'

I'm not sure how or why Frasier thought that Reg and Ron were different to any other. They were gangsters and murderers, which epitomises everything that he despises. Nevertheless, Frasier is a tough guy – a straight, tough guy.

Throughout our interview, he made his views on criminals crystal clear and insisted that he was not a hard bastard. We had a long discussion on what makes a hard bastard. We both agreed that bullies are not tough guys, they are just bullies. Some men are naturally tough, with an inner strength and sense of pride and dignity, like himself. He can't and won't for some reason let anyone push him around or take a liberty with him, but that doesn't make him a bully. Still, Frasier protested saying he wasn't a hard bastard.

At the photo-shoot later, Don the photographer asked Frasier to behave like he was in a strongman competition, to gesture angrily and shout. Frasier shouted for the camera and gritted his teeth, 'Come on! Come on!'

Everyone who was training in the gym stopped what they were doing and watched the big fella. Don continued to egg him on; Frasier responded. His eyes bulged. Purple veins in his neck swelled, pumping blood to his brain.

He grimaced. His face contorted with the effort. His eyes glistened with sweat. Two skinny lads watched from the back of the gym. One nudged the other, 'I wouldn't like to upset him. He's one Hard Bastard.'

NAME: Frasier Tranter.

DATE OF BIRTH: 17 November 1965.

STAR SIGN: Scorpio.

OCCUPATION: Proprietor of a security company and World Strongman contender.

BACKGROUND

I'm from Wolverhampton. I don't want to talk about my childhood. All I will say is that my parents were divorced and when I left school I had several menial jobs before starting work on the doors.

LIFE OF CRIME

I'm squeaky clean.

WEAPONRY

Being a strongman, I have to be strong all over. I can't have any weak points. My strength is in my back and shoulders.

TOUGHEST MOMENT

The biggest challenge of my life was in The World's Strongest Man competition in Morocco in 1998. I was a late entry and only had four weeks to prepare. Some guy from Denmark dropped out and I was put in at short notice. From the moment I stepped off the plane in Morocco, I felt intimidated by the other contestants. Their sheer size and strength was awesome. I didn't do very well, but at least I tried. Hopefully, I'll win The World's Strongest Man 2000.

IS THERE ANYONE YOU ADMIRE?

Martine McCutcheon – Tiffany from *EastEnders*. She's gorgeous. I'd give up everything for her.

DO YOU BELIEVE IN HANGING?

No, in case of mistakes. I believe people suffer more in prison. Take Myra Hindley as an example; I believe she has suffered more by being incarcerated for more than three decades.

IS PRISON A DETERRENT?

I don't know, I've never been. If people are a danger to society then they have to be segregated from it.

WHAT WOULD HAVE DETERRED YOU FROM A LIFE OF CRIME?

Prison. Any man that says prison is a 'doddle' is a fool.

WHAT MAKES A TOUGH GUY?

A man that can walk away from a fight rather than get involved.

FRASIER'S FINAL THOUGHT

I've been pushed to the limit several times and have lashed out. I don't particularly enjoy violence but I'm not going to stand there and be a punch bag for anyone. Some people look at me and think that because I'm big, I'm a target. Everybody has a tolerance level. Sometimes it's a long fuse and sometimes it's not. Every man has a limit and when you're pushed to that limit no matter how big or small you are, you will lash out. An angry man is a dangerous man!

HARD BASTARD

Errol Francis

ERROL FRANCIS

Meeting Errol Francis was an extraordinary experience. What did I expect? An awesome, frightening bodyguard perhaps? A larger-than-life, in-your-face bully type? Whatever I expected, what I actually got was a surprise. Quite a lot of surprises, actually.

The first thing that struck me was his shyness. Errol is an extremely modest and reserved man. He is smaller than I'd expected but much broader than I'd imagined. In actual fact, he's colossal – a whopping monster of a man. Even more of a surprise is that his size is natural. Errol doesn't use any growth-enhancing substances like steroids. His bulk is just the result of pure hard work and clean living. He's not a man who goes out boozing with his mates or womanising. Errol is a family man. His wife Sandra and their children come before anything or anybody. That was evident the first time I met him.

The other thing I didn't expect was his warmth. On our first brief meeting, he grabbed my hand and shook it like he really was genuinely pleased to see me, before ushering me into a room where 'we could talk'.

Errol found it difficult speaking about himself and his many achievements. I had to coax every single word from him. It was a long, drawn-out process and Errol said that he'd rather have had a tooth removed. He didn't want to seem a big-head or a braggart, but the truth is that Errol is the World Kick-Boxing Champion, he is Steven Spielberg's personal bodyguard and at the time he was contracted to Warner Bros looking after the stars on the film *Matrix*.

That's to name just a few of his accomplishments. But it hasn't always been an easy ride for Errol. His life has been a roller-coaster of turbulent twists and turns. He's a complex character full of deep, dark secrets still to be uncovered. There are parts of Errol's life that he is still unable to speak about. The things that have happened to him are just too painful for words. Errol has stared adversity in the face and overcome it through sheer hard work and determination. This is the reason why he is a hard bastard, and the most sought-after bodyguard both in this country and America. Cross him and you'll see why.

NAME: Errol Francis.

DATE OF BIRTH: 21 July 1956.

STAR SIGN: Leo, on the cusp with Cancer.

OCCUPATION: Celebrity minder.

BACKGROUND

I was born in Jamaica. I was five years old when I came to England. I went to live in Goose Green, East Dulwich in London. My father was the first black man to be a manager. It was a furniture shop in Brixton called Williams. At that time, most black men were either bus or train drivers but my father was always suited and booted. He had a good job and, on the surface of it, he was a good law-abiding citizen. But behind closed doors he was a tyrant and my worst enemy.

My dad had a saying: 'Bend a tree while it's young,' and that's what he tried to do with me. He beat me terribly.

I started going to the gym to let out some of my aggression and to get some attention. My trainer was the only man ever to say, 'Well done, Errol,' and I liked it. I started boxing and took up martial arts. At the time, Bruce Lee was popular and I'd go to late-night showings at the pictures and study his every move. At last I'd found a niche in life and the one thing I was good at – knocking people out, no argument.

I worked hard and I became the World Kick-Boxing Champion and a celebrity bodyguard. I now run the biggest club in South London and take kids off the street, training them to be British champions.

At the moment, I'm training for Mr Universe 2000. Training keeps my aggression in a safe place.

LIFE OF CRIME

Violence has always been part of my life – it's the only thing I really know. As a child growing up that's all I experienced and thought that's what adults did – bash each other up. I went from an approved school to a detention centre and then eventually to prison. All for violent crimes, inevitably ending in murder. I served six years inside but have been sentenced to ten.

WEAPONRY

I'm a great thinker. All my fights take place in my head first. So my mind is my greatest weapon.

TOUGHEST MOMENT

I've got to say preparation for any fight. I've always found that tough. Preparing to knock out an opponent or to defend myself. To gauge how hard to hit someone so as not to kill them. Just enough to maim, break a bone, knock out or stun. I think about every move carefully and will only hit someone according to what they have done to me.

IS THERE ANYONE YOU ADMIRE?

God. There is no one higher.

DO YOU BELIEVE IN HANGING?

Yes, I do for child abusers.

IS PRISON A DETERRENT?

No. It's a criminal breeding ground.

WHAT WOULD HAVE DETERRED YOU FROM A LIFE OF CRIME?

Nothing.

WHAT MAKES A TOUGH GUY?

Truth and being straight. A man can't be wrong and strong. If a person is wrong, he'll try and defend himself with his mouth but in his heart he has fuck all.

ERROL'S FINAL THOUGHT

When I was growing up I really thought that violence was how people got what they wanted. I now know that is rubbish. When I first came to this country, I was five years old. I stepped off the plane from Jamaica not knowing what to expect. For the first time I saw grey skies, big red buses and kids with ginger hair and freckles. I was told to eat with a knife and fork and was forced to wear shoes. All these things were alien to me. But the one thing that is universal, no matter where you come from or what colour you are, is: if you have a pound note then you have lots of friends and if you're a nice man people walk all over you. When you say, 'No more, man, I've had enough, I won't be beaten any more,' and retaliate, then I become the nutcase. Now I'm the bad guy.

HARD BASTARDS

The
Bowers

THE BOWERS

I'm waiting for the Bower brothers in the lounge of the Peacock Gym, east London, when it suddenly occurs to me that I might not recognise them – which would be really embarrassing. All I know is that they're three very good-looking brothers.

I'd heard about the Bowers many times, but I'd never actually met them. I'd heard that they were this and I'd heard that they were that, but mainly I'd heard that they were a family not to mess with; if you fuck with one then you take them all on! They don't flaunt themselves in public and they don't do the hard sell on the social scene – in fact, they are very private men.

As I waited for them to arrive, I looked around the gym and in particular at the many photos of young boxers hanging on the wall. There were photographs of youngsters and tearaways from the local neighbourhood whom they have encouraged and helped. There wasn't just one photograph, there were literally hundreds. The Peacock Gym is the most famous gym in London because it has the best facilities for the young and old.

A receptionist asked if she could be of any assistance; I said I was waiting for the Bower brothers. Then they appeared through a doorway, and I immediately experienced those penetrating, ridiculously brown, brown eyes probing the room. All three of them look like Hollywood film stars from a gangster movie.

Basically, it was male testosterone at its height – untamed charisma. Their shirts matched – silk and velvet – to complement their eyes and I wonder if it's a coincidence.

We moved to the patio for coffee or, in their case, weak tea. Every pair of female eyes in the room was glued to us. To put it into context, of all the people I've ever interviewed – murderers, gangsters and the hugely famous – I've never encountered such an outbreak of raw, female, slack-jaw lust.

The brothers took me to a palatial office on the top floor of the gym where we could talk in private. I switched on my tape recorder and placed it in between two posh desks. Tony Bowers sat behind one desk and Martin and Paul sat behind the other. They were polite and courteous throughout the interview, to me and to each other.

'Sorry, Tony, can I butt in there?' or 'If I can just interrupt you for a moment…'

They were young men with old-fashioned values who

rose to the occasion in their fine suits and silk ties embroidered with a certain dignity. They were rough diamonds. Then, with a tap on the door and a muffled 'Excuse me,' in walked their father, Wally. He is the figurehead of the family and probably the only man in the world who can control the three brothers. It was at that moment I realised where the brothers had inherited their manners and dignity from.

At first, the boys were eager to tell me about the things they do for the community and were as proud as peacocks that they were a registered charity.

That wasn't what I'd come to hear. I wanted blood and guts. I wanted to know if the fearsome reputation I'd heard about them was true. But with a wave of the hand and a flash of a pearly smile, my questions were dismissed.

They didn't need to say anything; the atmosphere, the mood and the feeling that they generated between themselves was enough to send a shiver down your spine.

Reluctantly, the boys agreed to be photographed for the book and I think the image speaks for itself.

NAME : Martin, Tony and Paul Bowers.

DATE OF BIRTH :

Tony: 15 August 1958.

Martin: 18 February 1965.

Paul: 8 March 1967.

STAR SIGN :

Tony: Leo.

Martin: Aquarius.

Paul: Pisces.

OCCUPATION : Entrepreneurs.

BACKGROUND

We were brought up in Canning Town, east London. We had a sister, Jayne Louise, but unfortunately she was killed.

I suppose you could say our dad Wally used to be a rascal. He's been inside a couple of times. When he was first put in prison our mum was very ill and she was always in and out of hospital so our dad's sister came to live with us. Tragically, our mum passed away. However, we still had lots of love, even though our dad was inside and Mum was no longer with us.

Us boys used to do the weekly shopping; we only had a couple of quid to do it each week but we never went short of anything. We'd put a big bag underneath the trolley and make our way round the supermarket. More things went in the bag than the trolley! We had to live by our wits which made us strong, helped us, drove us on if you like.

As kids we didn't do much schooling, we'd rather make camps and ours was always the best around. Whenever we built our camps we'd put everything in it. Every kid in the neighbourhood wanted to come to our camp and we carried that theory on in our businesses. If you put everything into it then people will want to join you. This lesson we have taken with us through our life. But we will never forget our background; we are street urchins and always will be.

LIFE OF CRIME
Who said we had a life of crime?

WEAPONRY
Not known to use anything.

TOUGHEST MOMENT
Losing our mother and sister.

IS THERE ANYONE YOU ADMIRE?
Our father Wally. He brought us up alone and that must have been a hard thing for a man to do in the Sixties.

DO YOU BELIEVE IN HANGING?
No. I think that all nonces should be kept in a building. When a sick or dying patient needs a new kidney or heart,

then the organs should be removed from the pervs. Don't just hang them – make use of them.

IS PRISON A DETERRENT?

No. Prison is a university and not a deterrent.

WHAT WOULD HAVE DETERRED YOU FROM A LIFE OF CRIME?

Money.

WHAT MAKES A TOUGH GUY?

A man who sticks by his family. Living by the rules. A man of his word. That's how you get respect: living by the rules.

THE BOWERS' FINAL THOUGHT

We've worked and worked for years. We've got lots of businesses – pubs, restaurants and cab firms. We've always worked. We've ducked and dived and done what we had to do to get to where we are today.

Nowadays, we try to put something back into the community instead of taking it out. We've got the biggest gym in London, The Peacock. We've got 12 football teams for children, we organise endless summer camps, amateur boxing competitions, UK Strongman, karate events, wrestling and marathons, to name but a few. It takes a lot of dedication and hard graft to keep our businesses afloat and we're lucky enough to have a good team of workers and helpers, both paid and voluntary.

Our greatest achievement is being a registered charity for the last six years. We can say hand on heart that there really is nothing like a 'straight pound note'.

HARD BASTARD

Glenn Ross

GLENN ROSS

Glenn Ross punched the air in triumph, 'I'm the Daddy,' he yelled.

That was the first time I saw Glenn. It was at the UK Strongman contest at the Peacock Gym in east London. Other contestants were strutting around in their designer gear – lycra shorts and skimpy vests. Glenn Ross was simply Glenn Ross. He has no time for such superficial trivia. He wore cut-down shorts and a baggy T-shirt.

There was something different about Glenn, something that set him above the rest. Not his size, as he was, without question, the biggest man there. It was the manner in which he conducted himself. He moved casually, smiled carefully and spoke slowly.

That day, Glenn won the title of the UK's Strongest Man. The next time I saw him was on TV in The World's Strongest Man. Glenn always stuck in my mind and I knew when I started this book that I wanted to find him. I contacted the Bower brothers who own the Peacock Gym; within minutes, Glenn was on the phone and within days I was on my way to Bangor, Northern Ireland, to interview him.

As I waited for Glenn to pick me up from the airport, I couldn't have prepared myself for how he looked. I had only ever seen him in shorts and T-shirts, so when he arrived fully dressed he was double the size. In fact, I had to look twice – he was absolutely gigantic.

I made the introductions to my minder and photographer. We crossed the car park to Glenn's car. He apologised that he had his baby son Marcus with him, as he gently strapped him into the baby seat. I looked at the car. I didn't think for one moment that we would all get in. The photographer climbed in the back with the baby and I climbed in with them. My minder sat in the front. When Glenn sat in the driver's seat, the car buckled under his 30-stone frame.

I looked at the back of his head. He hasn't got a neck, his head runs straight down to his shoulders. Everything about Glenn is big. His shoulders start underneath his ears and spread outwards like a rugged mountain. He is 30 stone of squat, solid muscle which ripples and bulges over his collar. His hands are like Spear and Jackson shovels.

At the time I interviewed him, Glenn was sporting a black eye. I asked him how he got it; he said that he had thrown a couple of trouble-makers out of a club in Belfast and had copped one in the eye. God knows what happened to the men he threw out!

That's just it; the way Glenn looks and the way he is are the complete opposite. I noticed the purple and red scars on his bulky forearms. I imagined that they were battle scars from fending off this blow or that. But they weren't. I was amazed to learn that Glenn used to be a pastry chef. The marks on his arms were scalds from a hot oven when he put the pastry and cakes in to cook. Life is full of surprises. It only confirms that you should never judge a book by its cover.

We arrived at Bangor Marina to do the interview. Everywhere we went, Glenn was recognised. People approached him and asked for an autograph or a photo for the album. Glenn is very approachable and eager to please and signed and posed with a smile. We took the photographs for the book on the dockside; then had lunch in a quaint restaurant overlooking the cold, bleak Irish sea.

We ate Irish mussels in garlic sauce while Glenn tenderly fed his baby son scrambled egg. He clucked and cooed over his offspring like a mother hen.

He was as proud as punch and didn't give a toss about trying to be macho or something that he wasn't. To me, his innocence was like a breath of fresh air.

Glenn wants to break into the world of show business. I suggested with caution that he enrol in the London-based agency called 'Ugly'. I didn't mean it in an offensive way and Glenn didn't take it that way. He was just pleased that I'd tried to help. When I got back to London, I signed him up with three agencies. When the agents for

Ugly saw the photographs of Glenn, they immediately put him on their books. Glenn was grateful for the help and chuffed to mint-balls when he got his first assignment.

He's currently training hard for the European and World Strongest Man competition. Glenn rubbed his hands gleefully.

'This is going to be my year. I'm going to be The World's Strongest Man 2000,' and with a wink and a smile, he added, 'Please God!'

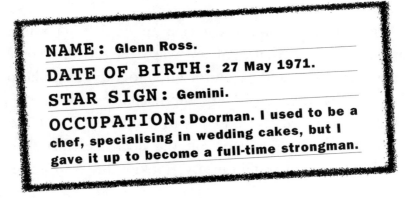

NAME: Glenn Ross.

DATE OF BIRTH: 27 May 1971.

STAR SIGN: Gemini.

OCCUPATION: Doorman. I used to be a chef, specialising in wedding cakes, but I gave it up to become a full-time strongman.

BACKGROUND

I am the eldest of two brothers and one sister. I weighed 9lb when I was born and was always big as a child. My father was a sales rep. Unfortunately, I no longer speak to my mother or father – I haven't done for ten years. I won't go into the details or reasons why we fell out, but let's just say it involved my granddad. So when I got married my granddad was the man on the top table at my reception, not my father.

Due to my dad's job, I spent a lot of my childhood in England, mainly in Warrington, Cheshire. Half my life

I've been to and from Warrington and Northern Ireland. That's probably why I love travelling. I'm not a good traveller though, as the seats are never big enough!

I left school when I was 16 to join the Boys' Service, which is a spring board into the Army. I did three years, Boys' Service and then signed up as a soldier for a further three years and trained to be a chef. It was in the Army that I first started physical training and I loved it. The Army turns you into a man but they also like to keep you a boy, with the control element, curfews and restrictions – I didn't like that. I wanted something different and left the Army at 21 and took up catering full time but continued with my training.

I won the All-Ireland Bodybuilding Championship and went on to win the UK Strongman and I haven't looked back since. In the year 2000, I aim to be the World Champion Strongman.

LIFE OF CRIME
My life has been spotlessly clean.

WEAPONRY
My greatest weapon is my size.

TOUGHEST MOMENT
My first job as a doorman was in a club called The Coach Inn, Belfast. In the past, the club had a lot of problems with drug dealers and paramilitaries. In my line of work, if I see two men fighting in the club I chuck them out, no questions, but, in Belfast, things are not that plain and

simple. Two men I chucked out of the club for fighting over drugs on a Saturday night were paramilitaries and they sanctioned a punishment beating on me.

It started off with the windows in my house being smashed. I came home from work to find my car burned out. I didn't want my family hurt, so I moved to a wee town outside Portadown, but they found out where I lived. I'd heard a whisper that something was going to happen so I had a crowbar hidden in my car.

November 1996. I finished work late; I was tired and all I wanted to do was get home to my wife Yvonne and have my dinner. I parked my car around the corner from my house. It was dark, no one was around. I didn't want to take my 'piece' home for my wife to see so I left it in my motor.

I locked the door and took two steps from the car. As I did, eight or ten guys ran from behind a row of garages. They were wearing boiler suits and brand-new balaclavas over their faces; they were real thick wool, I could see that in the light. I just remember thinking that this was it, I'm going to get fucking shot.

I knew there was a river behind me and I thought, well, guns can't swim, if I can make it across the river then I'll be all right. All I wanted to do was lead them away from my house, if they were going to kneecap me or shoot me in the back of the head then I didn't want my wife to witness it. I made a dash for a field behind me. It was pitch black. I ran across the field towards the river.

I could hear them chasing me. I weigh nearly 30 stone so I'm not the most athletic person in the world but I ran as fast as I could. Just before I hit the river, I fell down some kind of fucking hole, a rabbit or pot hole. As I tried to get up, I felt a blow to my head. I looked up and was surrounded by eight men holding pick-axe handles.

My first thought was, well, at least they're not going to shoot me, they're here to give me a beating. I just remember them swinging the pick-axe handles and bringing them down on my head again and again. I put my hands up to defend myself, but it was no good. The only thing I had in my defence was my size. I charged at one of them. I took a couple more blows round the head but managed to grab one of the pick-axe handles. I felt a couple more blows to my head; half-dazed, I lashed out. I swung the handle as hard as I could and brought it down on one of the attackers' heads. He screamed. I hit him again and again with all my might. I was bashing him out of sheer desperation – literally for my life. I couldn't see what I was hitting, blood was gushing down my face, but I could feel the guy on the floor. He wasn't moving. I started swinging the handle shouting, 'Come on, come on, you bastards.'

Two guys grabbed the man on the floor and started dragging him up the hill. I turned round; three or four guys were standing behind me. I wiped the blood from my eyes and waved the handle in the air.
'Come on then. Do you want some?'
They shit themselves and ran off. It was unbelievable, absolutely unbelievable, and I'll tell you now if they had stood for another two minutes they'd have finished me because my head was literally lying open. I waved the

pick-axe handle in the air shouting, 'Come back, you yellow bastards.'

As they disappeared out of sight, I remember saying to myself, 'Shut up, Glenn.' Then I collapsed. I had 60 staples in my head but at least I was alive.

IS THERE ANYONE YOU ADMIRE?

My granddad, because he was a war veteran. In my sport, I admire Bill Kazmire. He won the title of The World's Strongest Man and is the strongest man on the planet. On a personal level, I admire my wife Yvonne, for giving me my son and for putting up with me.

DO YOU BELIEVE IN HANGING?

Rapists and child abusers. They should definitely hang.

IS PRISON A DETERRENT?

No. In Northern Ireland, a prisoner hands in his 9mm Browning hand-gun and they are given a mobile phone. Also, they are allowed conjugal rights with their wives and prison officers can't go on to the landings. That's no punishment or deterrent.

WHAT WOULD HAVE DETERRED YOU FROM A LIFE OF CRIME?

I haven't been in trouble with the law and have never been to prison.

WHAT MAKES A TOUGH GUY?

Somebody who has respect from others and not fear. A

man who respects his family and puts them number one before all else, even before himself.

IS THERE ANYTHING TONY BLAIR COULD DO TO HELP PEACE?

I think that Tony Blair has done all in his power to help peace in Northern Ireland.

GLENN'S FINAL THOUGHT

Generally, I don't have any real regrets. I suppose I regret the way things have turned out with my family – my mum and dad and brothers and sister – but that's life, it's a decision I made. I am a firm believer in fighting for what you want. A man has to stand up and be counted, no matter who you are. It's better to stand tall than be small.

HARD BASTARD

John McGinnis

JOHN McGINNIS

What you see is what you get with John McGinnis. There are no frills, no pleasantries, just John. He doesn't dress to please or to impress, he's a man who is at peace with himself.

Usually when I'm doing an interview, it's either in a gym or a hotel or club, and I was surprised when John invited me to his house to talk to him. He lives in a quaint little village on the outskirts of Kent. It's an idyllic setting, with privet hedges and rose bushes. His home has a warm, cosy feel to it; John sat in John's chair with John's mug full of hot tea. Beside him were John's slippers and John's dog. It was blatantly obvious he's a creature of habit and dislikes change. I recognised that straight away.

John told me, 'I've been doing door work for 27 years. Girls are the worst you know. When women are in drink – they're murder. I've had them attack me, gob in my face,

157

then scream blue murder if I try to chuck 'em out.'

John is an old hand at door work. There's nothing you can tell him that he hasn't already seen. He's a master in his field. It's as comforting to him as his old worn armchair indoors.

I went to the club to see where he works. It was like a home from home. Just like in his front room, John sat in his usual spot – in John's chair, with John's newspaper and John's usual bottle of beer. He sits in the doorway reading his newspaper, barely bothering to look up at the young revellers coming into the club.

There's nothing in John's face to suggest that he is anything other than just a nice bloke. Until, that is, there's a disturbance inside the club. He reluctantly puts down his paper and beer and excuses himself. It's at that moment John's persona changes. The warm, friendly bloke disappears and out comes John's alter-ego – a nasty bastard. In a flash, the look in his eyes turns to hatred. I was amazed, it was such a turnaround. It was at that point that he was transformed into all the things that I'd heard about him: powerful, fiercely aggressive and dogmatic. And that's the reason why I just had to include him in *Hard Bastards*.

NAME: John McGinnis.

DATE OF BIRTH: 19 September 1954.

STAR SIGN: Virgo.

OCCUPATION: Doorman.

BACKGROUND

I was born in Woolwich, south London. My old man was always in and out of prison with a criminal record dating back to 1940. He was born in Northern Ireland, which is where it all started with minor burglaries. My dad was a wiry old fox and served twenty-one years of his life inside. He only weighed 13½ stone but, boy, could he have a fucking row! He was a drinker and it was the booze that killed him in the end.

He spent most of his life in England but, as with most Paddies, they all consider Ireland as home. When my dad was in hospital half dead from the ravages of drink, all he talked of was seeing Northern Ireland just once more. He made the journey home, but never made it back; he was buried in Northern Ireland.

While at the funeral I met cousins that I didn't even know existed. They were horse traders and tinkers, Paddies through and through, just like my dad.

Up until the age of 16 I lived in kids' homes, but it was one of my uncles that took me to work on a door. It never made me a millionaire, it just paid for the groceries.

LIFE OF CRIME

I've been inside once and once was enough. I got three years for a violent attack.

WEAPONRY

I've always got a 'piece' in the back of the motor and anyone that hasn't I think is a fool. When I have a row I don't use it every time, but I know it's there – just in case.

TOUGHEST MOMENT

Call me superstitious, but I've always had a thing about door work and I've never looked after a pub or club unless I knew for certain it was going to be long term. All the places I've looked after have always been long-term contracts, including the one I'm at now. It's been seven years and Woolwich before that was thirteen. If I'm going to sort out a club and make it safe by putting my life on the line, then it's got to be a good earner for me. I've got to stamp my mark from the outset and if that means having a row then so fucking be it.

I've had lots of confrontations that can sometimes spill over as an offshoot from my door work.

I'd had a little run in on a Friday night with some 'herberts'. They were boozed up and playing up. I slung them out of the club – simple as that. Later in the evening, my friend came in and said that he'd seen them hanging around outside. He said he thought they were carrying something. I went outside to have a look and before I knew it I was being shot at. One of the bullets missed me by a fraction. It was a very, very dodgy night!

IS THERE ANYONE YOU ADMIRE?

People that are loyal to each other and don't grass. Oh, and anybody that gets one over on the Old Bill!

DO YOU BELIEVE IN HANGING?

I think that certain people deserve to be hanged. There are two kinds of murderers: if a couple of geezers are having a row in a pub and one bloke dies, that's just bad luck.

Then there are people like paedophile Sidney Cook. They are the scum of the earth. I'd hang them from the nearest tree.

IS PRISON A DETERRENT?

Not when you're younger but it is when you're older. When I did my 'bird' I was double fit and could handle it but when you're older you've got more to lose.

The worst thing for me was when my wife came to visit me every two weeks with the kids. They were only babies and the hardest thing for me was to watch them walk out of the prison. It's such a fucking waste of time but you've just got to get on with it.

WHAT WOULD HAVE DETERRED YOU FROM A LIFE OF CRIME?

I'm not saying that I don't do things illegal but I wouldn't do them full time. The thing that deters me now is more 'bird'.

WHAT MAKES A TOUGH GUY?

Not getting beaten up locally. I might go on holiday to a Greek Island and get a chair whacked over my head but no one knows about it. If you get stuck on your arse on your doorstep by someone, your respect and reputation flies straight out of the window. A real hard bastard is someone who can take a hiding, and give one.

JOHN'S FINAL THOUGHT

I think drugs have changed things today. It's made

everyone a lot slimier. They bring out the worst in everyone. I see it every night I'm working on the door. It could be the skinniest of kids but when he's out of his head he'd think nothing of stabbing or shooting you. They think they're invincible. It's a shame but it's the way of the world today.

HARD BASTARD

Felix Ntumazah

FELIX NTUMAZAH

If it was legal to carry a gun, would you feel safe? If you could walk to the shops with a samurai sword strapped to your back, or be trained as a black belt in karate, would you feel more confident that no one would think of attacking you?

Let's say you were armed to the teeth, and walking along minding your own business. Maybe you turn a corner and, from nowhere, you are attacked, by three members of the local boot, beer and drug club. One of the slags grabs you by the throat, pushes you against a wall and wants to 'kill the black bastard'. What would you do? Would you shoot one of your attackers with the Magnum; cut the second to pieces with your sword; then treat the third to a damn good beating? The Magnum is still asleep in your pocket; the last thing the sword cut was your finger; you could beat him to a pulp with your bare hands if only he'd let go of your throat.

Felix Ntumazah has found himself in all of these situations and has handled each one successfully. But Felix is not a villain, gangster or hardened criminal in any way, shape or form. He is a straight guy.

In fact, Felix is an intelligent sophisticated man that studied his O-Levels in both French and English. He is a trained accountant and surveyor. He also speaks fluent French, English, Albanian, Arabic and Lingala, the language of Zaïre.

Perhaps by now you are asking yourself, why is he included in a book called *Hard Bastards*? Simple – he is one of the most dangerous men in this country. A wolf in sheep's clothing. It's not written in stone anywhere that you have to be a bad guy to be a tough guy; and Felix is a tough guy all right. Not only is he a black belt in karate, he also holds the title of British Champion. But, moreover, he commands the utmost respect from whoever he meets. His reputation preceeds him wherever he goes, but tread on his toes and you'll wish to God you hadn't.

Whatever Felix sets his mind to, he is totally focused and dedicated until he achieves his goal.

I'd heard about this mysterious straight guy with an awesome reputation and wanted to meet him. I managed to track him down at Crystal Palace sports centre, South London, where he was teaching youngsters karate. As I interviewed Felix, I found him to be a shrewd judge of character, and not tolerant of excuses.

His eyes were as black as coal, his voice barely a whisper, but a controlled threat of violence engulfed him.

In his spare time, Felix also does security on troublesome clubs around London. He doesn't need the money, so why does he do it, I asked him.

'Fighting has always been part of my life. The thrill. The buzz. There ain't nothing like it. I guess it goes back to the palaeolithic age, when men lived in caves and were primitive and brutal. The hunter. The protector. The victor. I'm a man – aggression is natural, and I love it!'

NAME: Felix Ntumazah.

DATE OF BIRTH: 29 August 1962.

STAR SIGN: Virgo.

OCCUPATION: British Karate Champion.

BACKGROUND

There are nine of us in my family: six girls and three boys. I'm number six. My parents were into politics. My dad was a politician. He was the leader of the opposition in Cameroon, where my parents are from. I was brought up in different countries. I was born in Ghana and when I was about six months old I went to Albania and I lived there for five years. From there I went to the Congo for five years and Algeria for five years before I came to the UK.

Looking back, my childhood was OK, but at the time I didn't think so. I thought it was pretty hard because of political pressures. My dad was sought after by various governments in Cameroon. They didn't like his political ideas.

I'd been to a French school all my life, so when I came to the UK I had to go to school for a year to learn how to speak English. Then after that I went to college to do my O-levels again. I'd done them in French but I had to re-do them in English.

English was difficult to comprehend. I did all that in my first year and then I went on to do accountancy. But martial arts is the love of my life.

I am the British Karate Champion. I've won the British championship five times in a row. It's a full-contact, knock-down tournament. The aim is to try and knock your opponent out. I am a black belt, three stripes.

LIFE OF CRIME

I haven't been to prison or had a life of crime as such. I think I've just been lucky, I haven't been caught. As a kid in Algeria I ran with a gang – over there, using razors and knives is part of daily life. I've been stabbed and shot when I was young. Karate hasn't mellowed me, I've got to say I enjoy fighting.

WEAPONRY

My legs are dangerous weapons.

TOUGHEST MOMENT

When I was in Algeria, my stepfather was beaten almost half to death by a gang. The gang were cowards. First, they let down my stepfather's tyres on his car. As he bent down to fix them, they hit him on the head, then kicked and punched him for no reason. When he came home bleeding, I saw red. I found out where his attackers lived and went to seek revenge. As I approached the house, shots were fired from the window.

I fell to the ground unable to move, while being shot at from every angle. I'd say it was one of the stickiest moments of my life.

IS THERE ANYONE YOU ADMIRE?
Muhammad Ali. He epitomises everything I would like to stand for, on issues like racism and fighting for the cause of the poor and under-privileged.

DO YOU BELIEVE IN HANGING?
No, I don't. It's too barbaric. By hanging someone they're not necessarily going to die straight away. I believe in capital punishment but not hanging. I'd prefer to shoot someone or give them a lethal injection, it's far more civilised.

IS PRISON A DETERRENT?
No. My family were imprisoned for political reasons. For the people I know it hasn't acted as a deterrent, on the contrary, it made them worse. When they came out of prison they thought they could rule the world.

WHAT WOULD HAVE DETERRED YOU FROM A LIFE OF CRIME?
As a child I was faced with a lot of racism. When I lived in Albania there were very few black people and being

black was a novelty. It wasn't racism so much as ignorance. Black people have to try and adapt to different situations. The times I've been in trouble have nearly always been down to racism.

If someone abuses me now I will only respond if that person should intellectually know better – then I become violent. If it's just someone shouting, 'You black so and so,' then I know it's just sheer ignorance. I've heard it said many times – the reason why there is a lot of unemployment is because black people take all the jobs. That's sheer ignorance. If an intellectual person says the same thing then I'd probably become aggressive because they should know better.

WHAT MAKES A TOUGH GUY?

Toughness is within. Stand your ground and people will respect you.

FELIX'S FINAL THOUGHTS

I have the reputation of being very calculating and calm. I don't fly off the handle but that doesn't mean I'm weak. If you cross me I will always come after you.

I was attacked by a gang of skinheads in Tooting just because I was black. I was cornered in an alley and surrounded. They were spitting and shouting obscenities at me. In my eyes they were cowards, unable to fight me one on one. They were all pushing and shoving me and then someone hit me on the head. From the first blow there was no stopping them, they were like sharks when they got the smell of blood.

First one punched me, then another one kicked me. I

felt my lip split and my nose break, then the ringleader grabbed me and pushed me against the wall. He pulled a knife from his pocket and stuck it to my throat. I saw the hatred in his eyes. His mates egged him on, 'Kill him, cut the black bastard.'

I stared into his eyes as the tip of the knife pierced my skin, I whispered, 'You can cut me, but you'd better kill me or I'll come after you.'

For a moment I saw his eyes change. He was no killer, just a bully trying to be flash in front of his mates. He didn't have the courage to kill me; I saw it in his eyes. It takes a lot to kill a man – even a black man.

HARD BASTARD

Bobby Wren

BOBBY WREN

No one will ever get to the bottom of Bobby Wren. I can't fathom out whether he's SAS, ex-military, mercenary or just a dangerous bastard. He's an odd-bod, a loner. A modest, reserved enigma. Bobby is gadget mad and has sophisticated paraphernalia for just about everything.

I sat in Spencers pub in Hornchurch, Essex, waiting to interview Bobby – he was late. My minder ordered me another orange juice from the bar while I fiddled with my tape recorder. I glanced at my watch and thought to myself, I'll give him another five minutes. At that moment, the saloon door burst open and in scurried Bobby Wren suited and booted, carrying a hold-all. He was sweating profusely and apologised for being late. I asked him if he'd been running for a bus or something. He scowled, 'I've just finished training!'

By the size of him, he wasn't kidding. His shoulders are so broad he could carry the weight of the whole world on them.

During our interview, Bobby showed me up-to-date heat-seeking equipment, bugging devices, and a gadget that he wears on his chest that vibrates if someone close to him is armed. While I was with him he wanted to demonstrate 60 ways to break a man's arm in under a minute – I declined.

Bobby is a strange, complex character who holds his cards close to his chest – probably next to the vibrating gadget!

I've known Bobby for some years but the incident about him that sticks out in my mind most happened when Ron died.

I stood by the freshly dug grave. The vicar stood at one end, 'Ashes to ashes, dust to dust ...'

Something distracted me. I glanced over my shoulder. A man dressed in combat clothes, wearing a woolly hat and carrying a gun appeared from behind a gravestone. His eyes bulged. He fixed me with a steely gaze. He winked and disappeared as quickly as he had arrived – it was Bobby Wren. I later learned that he'd staked out the graveyard three days before the funeral. I don't know what he thought was going to happen, but in a macabre way it was comforting knowing someone was watching out for me.

Bobby took a lot of persuading to be included in this book and, even when he finally agreed, he was very reluctant to talk about the things he'd been involved in.

What intrigued me about Bobby was the mystery hold-all that was his constant companion. It was a large blue canvas bag with lots of zips and compartments. It was full to bursting and Bobby is very secretive about what it contains.

From time to time during the interview, Bobby would delve into the mystery hold-all and produce some gadget or other, or a bulging file containing top-secret information on this person or that. I noticed George Harrison's name on the top of one of the files. This was shortly after the attempted murder of the ex-Beatle.

I asked Bobby if it was his security company that had been assigned to look after George. Bobby paused and threw me a look, a Bobby Wren look, a look of contempt, a 'how dare you?' look. Instinctively, I knew not to pursue the matter any further.

At the end of the interview, Bobby excused himself to use the toilet. He picked up his mystery hold-all and placed it precariously on the table in front of me. I wanted to have a peek inside but remembered the old saying, 'curiosity killed the cat'.

I restrained the urge to have a rummage in the hold-all, got up from my seat and approached the bar to speak to my minder and photographer. Out of the corner of my eye, I noticed Bobby Wren standing in the doorway, furtively spying through the window at me. What was he expecting to see? Perhaps he was waiting for me to go through his hold-all? I noticed the bag was positioned very carefully and remembered that he'd moved the ashtray and some empty glasses on the table to position his concealed bag of tricks. It was then I asked myself, was there a surveillance camera or bugging device in the mystery hold-all? Was he testing or listening? I'll probably never know.

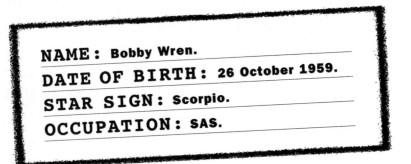

NAME: Bobby Wren.

DATE OF BIRTH: 26 October 1959.

STAR SIGN: Scorpio.

OCCUPATION: SAS.

BACKGROUND

I was born and brought up in Crystal Palace. One of five children. That's all I'm prepared to say.

LIFE OF CRIME

I do have convictions, but I'd rather not say what they are.

WEAPONRY

My arms and legs are my deadliest weapons. I also have a class five firearms licence.

TOUGHEST MOMENT

Not prepared to say.

IS THERE ANYONE YOU ADMIRE?

No.

DO YOU BELIEVE IN HANGING?

No, 'cos there but for the grace of God go I.

IS PRISON A DETERRENT?

No. Prison is a demoralising waste of time. You leave your morals and dignity at the gate when you go in, and pick them up on the way out. But something has to be done to keep law and order.

WHAT WOULD HAVE DETERRED YOU FROM A LIFE OF CRIME?

I'm straight. What I do is in self defence.

WHAT MAKES A TOUGH GUY?

An honest man. Someone who can hold his head up with dignity.

BOBBY'S FINAL THOUGHT

Violence is my job. It's what I do best. I'm not bragging or trying to be flash, that's just the way it is. I'm dedicated to my profession – I have to be to stay alive. I've been trained in 18 different martial arts; I've been taught to disarm a man whilst blindfolded; I can show you 60 ways to break your arm and pressure points that can bring a man to his knees in seconds. It's hard to describe my job. It hasn't got an exact label, or title. Some say – SAS. Others say mercenary.

I can't, for legal and security reasons, elaborate on the things that I've been involved in, but the dictionary definition of mercenary is a man hired to fight and kill solely for money. I guess that sums me up.

HARD BASTARD

Ronnie Field

RONNIE FIELD

Ronnie is a man who changes his moods as swiftly as a chameleon changes its colour. He doesn't pander to whims but is a force to be reckoned with. He demands respect. A commander of men.

Ronnie is always immaculately dressed in starched white shirts and well-cut suits, which projects an image of respectability; but cross him, and he will fight like a devil.

He's currently residing in one of 'Her Majesty's big houses'. That's a polite way of saying he's banged up in the slammer – nine years for intent to supply cocaine.

I've known Ron for 11 years. He was my minder while I was married to Ronnie. There are so many stories I could tell you about Ronnie Fields. Some are funny, some are frightening and some are sinister. But I can't tell you any of these for obvious reasons. I would if I could, but I can't so I won't.

During the time I've known Ron, he's been to prison a couple of times; he never complains or makes a song and dance about being sent down.

It's just a hazard of his profession – armed robbery. But the sentence he's serving at the moment is different. I know for a fact that Ron is not a drug baron, never has been and never will be. It's just not his bag. The way he was treated stinks! It should be illegal.

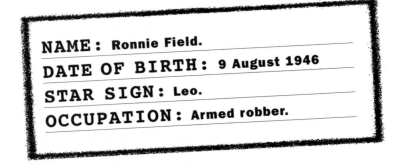

NAME: Ronnie Field.

DATE OF BIRTH: 9 August 1946

STAR SIGN: Leo.

OCCUPATION: Armed robber.

BACKGROUND

I was born in Epsom, Surrey, the youngest of seven children. My father was a safe-blower who learned his trade in the Army. He was a highly decorated soldier at the D-Day landings and crossing of the Rhine. Dad left home when I was four years old. Me and my brothers were left with my grandmother – she was a tyrant. I was lucky she left me alone.

LIFE OF CRIME

1976 – I was sentenced to 12 years for an armed robbery on a wages office in Leeds. I got another ten years for an armed robbery on a supermarket in Wimbledon. In 1991,

I was arrested at Gatwick airport for conspiracy to commit armed robbery – estimated value, £10 million. I was sentenced to five years for that one!

1996 – Me, Charlie Kray and one other were arrested by undercover police for supplying cocaine. I received nine years, Charlie Kray received 12, the other mate five years. I'm guilty of the other armed robberies; I'll put my hands up to those, it was a fair cop! But for supplying cocaine, I know the truth. The whole thing stank from start to finish. The fucking thing felt like entrapment, which is no defence in this country, although it is in every other European state.

I'll do the nine years standing on my head, but it's wrong, plain and simple. I'm not saying this because I'm trying to get out of my sentence, because I've nearly completed it. I'm saying it because it is wrong. There's a word which means 'to catch or snare in a trap', and that's just what happened to me, Charlie Kray and a mate.

WEAPONRY
See no evil, hear no evil, speak no evil.

TOUGHEST MOMENT
My toughest moment was when my mother died and I didn't get a chance to say sorry for all the worry I'd given her. Also, the day my baby daughter died was probably my darkest hour.

IS THERE ANYONE YOU ADMIRE?
I don't know if 'admire' is the right word, but probably

the only man I'd trust with my life is Joey Pyle. He is a man of honour and one I respect.

DO YOU BELIEVE IN HANGING?

Yes, for sex offenders and killers of children. There is no cure and they never change, despite what doctors and do-gooders say. In prison, the nonces and ponces are mollycoddled as if they are sick. They're sick all right – sick in the fucking head. They don't need help, they need stringing up.

IS PRISON A DETERRENT?

I suppose prison is a deterrent to a certain extent. Nobody wants to go to prison and the older you get, the more of a deterrent it becomes.

WHAT WOULD HAVE DETERRED YOU FROM A LIFE OF CRIME?

Dough, loot, moolah, lolly, spondulix – what else?

WHAT MAKES A TOUGH GUY?

A man who shouts from the rooftops telling everyone that he's bashed this one and bashed that one or killed this one and killed that one – he is nothing but a fool. It's the quiet, unobtrusive man that is dangerous.

RONNIE'S FINAL THOUGHT

I should have sussed it. I should have sussed his boots – black, polished Dr Martens.

To tell the truth, I had been clean for a while; I never

intended to do any more 'work'. I wanted to spend some quality time with my daughter Sadie and my grandson and just have a rest.

I didn't want any more 'cozzers' kicking my door open in the middle of the night. I'm not saying that I was ready for pipe and slippers, but I wanted to take a back seat – at least for a while.

From time to time, I'm asked to go to 'work' with this one or that. Usually, I stick to my own, never venturing away from the people I know and trust. Then, out of the blue, I got a call from someone I knew, but wasn't a friend. He explained about a job that he was involved in. It sounded good – fucking good. He offered me a bit of the action and I've got to admit I was tempted. Foolishly, I decided to meet the men offering the 'bit of work'. Well, it couldn't hurt just meeting them.

Arrangements were made to meet in a quiet pub on the outskirts of London. The pub was unfamiliar to me – it was out of my manor. I should have just turned round and walked away, but I didn't. Instead, I ordered a round of drinks and listened. I said nothing, just listened. From the outset, I didn't like the set-up. I had a gut feeling, something just wasn't right. I felt a bit uncomfortable but pushed it to the back of my mind.

There was talk of kilos and kilos of cocaine. £10 million, £15 million, £22 million pounds' worth of charlie. It was rootin', tootin' big time and not my scene. I told 'em to count me out. But the boys were nothing if not persistent.

All sorts of outlandish figures were bandied around.

I'm not a mug, I've been up to skullduggery for as long as I can remember. I'm not sure if the boys persuaded me or I convinced myself that the job was a good idea. The more I listened, the more I began to wobble.

'How easy? How much?'

I thought to myself that if I did this one, the big 'un, then I could settle down and behave myself – for good!

I asked my mate how well he knew the other blokes. With a wave of his hand, he dismissed the question, 'Oh, I've known them for years. They're kosher ...'

I looked at their tanned faces and false smiles. The Armani suits. The Rolex watches. The flash cars. They had all the trappings. It was at that point I noticed their boots. I suspiciously asked, 'You ain't Old Bill, are ya?'

They were cool. Inside, they must have been dying. I should have gone with my gut feeling and got my sorry arse out of there. I didn't.

If I can pass on anything from my experiences to a young, up-and-coming villain, it's this: always judge a man by his shoes. If he wears worn, black, polished Dr Marten boots, then tell him in no uncertain terms to 'fuck off'. Because make no mistake – he's Old Bill.

HARD BASTARD

Reggie Parker

REGGJE PARKER

'Call security. Call security,' squealed the barmaid.

Reg sneered, 'I am fucking security.'

It was Saturday night in a nightclub on the outskirts of London. By chance that afternoon I had been interviewing Reg for this book. His mobile phone rang. Reg scowled.

'Fucking Tom. I'll be there later,' he hissed.

'Trouble Reg?' I asked.

'Nothing I can't handle, Kate. I've got an idea. Why don't you come with me to the club tonight and see how I run things?'

Tom was the owner of the nightclub and had taken a liberty. Reg Parker was going to 'sort it'.

Later that night, the club was packed. Reg leaned on the bar, saying, 'Sorry you've got to witness this, Kate, but business is business.'

I smiled, shrugged my shoulders and took a sip from the ice-cold drink that Reg handed me. The club was full. Reg cordoned off one side of the bar. With just a look, everyone instantly knew not to wander into his territory. The barmaid phoned for assistance, 'I need help in the bar area,' she squealed in a cockney accent.

Five burly doormen all dressed in black swung into action. Trouble at last, someone to sling out of the club. That's what they had been waiting for all night. They puffed out their chests and elbowed their way through the dancers. As they approached the bar they saw Reg pulling the top off a bottle of beer. The doormen stopped in their tracks.

'All right, Reg?' they called.

'Yeah, I'm just fine and fucking dandy,' he laughed.

The doormen knew from experience that if Reg was in the club on a Saturday night that meant only one thing – trouble. The fire in Reggie's eyes said it all. Even though the doormen worked for Reg, they knew when he was in a bad mood, he was dangerous and someone was going to cop it. Word soon buzzed around that Reg was in the club. Tom, the owner, was sitting in his office when one of his side-kicks scurried in.

'Reg is in tonight, Tom, what are we going to do?'

Tom buried his head in his hands and sighed. If Reg was in the club, it meant that he had found out that Tom had used other doormen in one of his other clubs. Reg would go ballistic and he knew it.

Reg had looked after Tom's interests for 15 years. Tom had gone into the club business without a clue of how things worked. It had been a nightmare from start to finish. Every night was the same; gypsies from the local campsite had taken over his club, smashed the place up, drank what they wanted, refused to pay and then terrorised anyone they didn't like the look of.

Tom was at his wit's end and had to take drastic action, he had to take control. But how? Then he heard about Reg Parker from a friend.

'Parker will sort your club out. He is the man. But it will cost ya.'

Tom didn't care. He wanted his club back, whatever the price.

'How do I get hold of this Reg Parker?' Tom asked.

'You don't. He gets hold of you,' came the reply.

Within days, Reg was at the club. Tom begged Reg to help him. Reg was cool. It was the same old story – gypsies. He'd heard it a dozen times. Reg didn't want to know the details and interrupted Tom.

'It will cost ya £300 a week, and I have my own men on the door.'

Tom didn't hesitate. 'Fine ... Fine ... When can you start?'

On the Thursday night, Reg assembled five of his most trusted men, and all were armed. Reg stood outside the door of the club. Nervous anticipation filled the air. Clubbers started to arrive. Reg studied everyone who came through the door. The doormen searched them carefully. Tom was nowhere to be seen, he was pacing around his cluttered office. Anxiously, he glanced at his watch. It was just after 11.30pm. The pubs were throwing out. Tom knew it wouldn't be long before the trouble started. He was right.

A taxi pulled up outside the club and three men got out. They were drunk, laughing loudly. One unzipped his trousers and relieved himself alongside the entrance to the club. Reggie's eyes narrowed. His hand tightened around a baseball bat. Fucking liberty, he thought.

It was obvious the three were gypsies from the local campsite. Their gold sovereign rings and dealer boots set them apart from the trendy clubbers. Reg hated gypsies. He'd had dealings with them before.

He considered them no-good bullies and Reg won't stand bullies. He leaned across the doorway blocking their entrance.

'You ain't coming in,' he snarled.

The gypsies looked at each other and laughed. 'Who's gonna stop us?'

Reg stood his ground. The atmosphere was electric. 'I am.'

The biggest of the group stepped forward. He looked Reg straight in the eye. Reg didn't blink. Their eyes locked in mortal combat.

The gypsy was a big man in his late thirties, a tough bastard, his rugged face scarred from previous fights. Reg never moved a muscle. The gypsy lost his nerve.

'We'll be back,' he hissed.

Reg nodded. He knew they would be back, only this time mob-handed. Reg didn't have to wait long.

In no time at all, a beaten-up white transit van arrived outside the club. A dozen men climbed from the back. All were carrying pieces of wood and iron bars. Reg was incensed. How dare they?

Reggie rushed out of the club and smashed the ring leader over the head with his baseball bat. He dropped to his knees. Blood trickled down his face. Another gypsy attacked Reg. CRACK, Reg bashed him, too. Then another ... then another. All hell broke loose. Reg yelled from the top of his voice, 'Stay the fuck away – I run this club now.'

It took two months of fighting, night after night. The gypsies tried everything. But Reg was too strong. Anyone who was sent to the club to hurt Reg was bashed – bad. Word on the street soon spread that Reg Parker had the door.

For 15 years, it has been Reggie's name that has kept trouble away from the club. Now Tom wanted to use other doormen. Well, it doesn't work like that. When you acquire someone like Reg Parker, you acquire him for life, as Tom was about to find out.

Tom pushed his way through the crowd, his mind racing. He had to convince Reg that he hadn't taken a liberty. Reg stood at the bar.

'All right, Reg – everything OK?'

Reg didn't look at Tom, in fact he never even acknowledged his presence. Nervously, Tom asked again, 'Reg, everything OK?'

Reg held up his finger to hush Tom from speaking.

'I'll see you in your office at 2.00am.'

Tom knew what that meant.

'But, Reg ... Reg ...'

'2.00am. Your office. Now fuck off.'

With a wave of a finger, Tom was dismissed.

For the rest of the evening, Reg continued to drink free beer.

At 2.00am the lights went on. Tipsy girls in short skirts collected their coats. Snogging couples were ushered out of dark corners. Still Reg leaned on the bar drinking. One of the doormen tried to escort a drunk out.

'Punch him in the throat and sling him down the stairs,' Reg laughed.

The man was either pissed or demented because he shouted, 'Come and do it yourself, if you think you're hard enough.'

Reg smirked and winked. He strode across the dance floor. His huge fist, the size of a club hammer, clenched. CRACK! Reg smashed the drunk in the throat. He let out a gasp. Reg hissed, 'I'll smash the granny out of you, you mother-fucker.'

To the disgust of onlookers, Reg picked the man up like a rag doll and dragged him to the top of the stairs. The drunk was a big strong man and tried to fight back, but he didn't stand a chance. When they reached the top of the stairs, Reg kicked him in the back, sending him hurtling to the bottom, which he reached with a thud. Still Reg wasn't finished.

He ran down the stairs and jumped on the man's head, then kicked him in the face. The other doormen pulled Reg off, shouting, 'That's enough … that's enough.' Reg shrugged his shoulders. 'Where's Tom?'

Tom was hiding in his office. He was counting the

night's takings, trying to look busy. Reg walked in and locked the door.

'I'll gouge your fucking eyes out ...'

From that night on, Tom paid an extra £100 a week and never brought in outside doormen again.

I interviewed Reg at great length for this book and, without doubt, he is a force to be reckoned with. Every day Reg wrestles with the good and evil sides of his nature. What I witnessed that night in the club, and particularly when I saw Reg angry, was a man on the brink of madness. As a friend, Reg is a good one, but make an enemy of him and it will be at your peril.

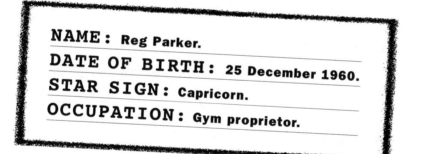

NAME : Reg Parker.

DATE OF BIRTH : 25 December 1960.

STAR SIGN : Capricorn.

OCCUPATION : Gym proprietor.

BACKGROUND

I was born in Abbey Wood, South London, but my family moved to Kent when I was ten years old. Mind you, as soon as I was able to drive I moved back to London. I'm the youngest of five boys. The biggest influence in my life was my granddad, Reginald Boxhall Prigmore. He was a generous, gentle man, a bank manager, of all things. He worked for the Bank of England and of New Zealand.

That's where my nicer side comes from. The other side of me, the nasty side, comes from my father. All five of us boys were frightened of my dad. He ruled us with a rod of iron. Mum tried to tell us off and hit us with broomsticks. But we just laughed.

I started training at an amateur boxing club in Abbey Wood before I was ten years old. But my father didn't like me boxing and put a stop to it. But not for long and soon I was back in London, where I got involved in unlicensed fighting. In the early days, I'd get in the ring and have a tear-up.

But I soon sussed out there was more money in promoting. One of the biggest promotions I staged was a bout between Lenny McLean and Gypsy Joe Bradshaw.

LIFE OF CRIME

All my arrests have been for violence, but I've never been to prison.

WEAPONRY

I use my fists, but ... but ...

TOUGHEST MOMENT

In 1994, I was sent to the 'nut-house'. I wasn't well in my head. I didn't like being there, I didn't like it one bit, and managed to escape. When I was captured, I was sectioned. The doctors started giving me lots of drugs, but I wouldn't co-operate. So they had no option but to strap me down and inject me. My body had spasms, I didn't know where I was or even who I was. My jaw locked, and

I was unable to speak. If it wasn't for my brother visiting me, I would be dead – there's no doubt about that.

IS THERE ANYONE YOU ADMIRE?

My mum; it must have been tough bringing up five boys.

DO YOU BELIEVE IN HANGING?

Yes, all paedophiles should be hanged. No ifs, buts or maybes. If they interfere with kids – string 'em up.

IS PRISON A DETERRENT?

No. When you're 'at it', you never think you're gonna get caught.

WHAT WOULD HAVE DETERRED YOU FROM A LIFE OF CRIME?

Fuck all!

WHAT MAKES A TOUGH GUY?

Brawn and brains. You've got to know when to start and when to stop; you've got to be able to read a situation.

REG'S FINAL THOUGHT

I don't trust anyone. I think a man is lucky if, in his lifetime, he has a handful of close friends. Some say I'm paranoid. Maybe I am. But I think, in my world, being paranoid ain't a bad thing. Nowadays, it seems everyone's out for themselves. There's no loyalty or trust. I put that down to drugs and money. The two go hand in hand. Greed.

Drugs have changed the face of crime all over the world. When someone is out of his head, he doesn't know what the fuck he's doing. I run most of the doors on nightclubs around South London so I see things first hand. I know what I'm talking about. It's a dog-eat-dog world. The Bible says, 'Do unto others before they do unto you.' I translate that to mean, 'They're all wankers so smash the fucking granny out of them.'

HARD BASTARD

Cass
Pennant

CASS PENNANT

Close your eyes and imagine it's the late Eighties; you're in the King's Road near Stamford Bridge; there's a football match between Chelsea and West Ham. It's a London Derby – East v West. Trouble is expected from the notorious Inter-City Firm (ICF), Britain's most feared gang of soccer hooligans. The threat of violence fills the air. National Front skinheads roam the streets wearing boots, braces, Fred Perrys and denims. All with close-cropped hair, all pug-uglies, chanting and clapping, 'East London, East London...'

Cass Pennant's name had been mentioned to me a few times during my research for *Hard Bastards*. First from the Bowers, then from Stilks. I'd heard a lot about him and his awesome reputation and I just had to meet him. Stilks telephoned me and gave me his number and we arranged to meet at The Bull Inn, South London.

It was early evening on a rainy night in mid-January. I arrived at the pub. I thought the rain would have stopped by now, but it hadn't. I locked my car door, ducked my head against the chill wind and dashed into the pub. As I did, I noticed a gold Mercedes parked up on the pavement with a private plate.

I thought, Well, at least he's on time. I hadn't a clue what Cass looked like and, to be honest, I never gave it a thought until I was actually walking through the door.

I glanced round the bar. There was a fat man perched precariously on a stool – nah, that wasn't him. A scruffy man in dirty working boots sipped a pint of Guinness – nah, that wasn't him either.

Standing at the bar, ordering half a lager, was a 7ft smartly-dressed black man. He wore a full-length Burberry macintosh and was carrying an attaché case; an important-looking folder bulging with official papers was safely tucked under his arm. Nah, it couldn't be him … could it? With much trepidation, I approached the man. I felt awkward. What was I going to say?

'Are you the hard bastard?'

Sensing my hesitation, Cass put his hand out. 'You must be Kate?'

I laughed. 'Well, knock me down with a fucking feather. You ain't what I expected, ain't what I expected at all.'

That's just it, Cass Pennant is a Pandora's box full of surprises. In the past, he was Harold Wilson's minder, of all things. He also saved a 'brother' from a beating on an afternoon train; the 'brother' was Frank Bruno.

I've got to say that Cass is the most unlikely-looking football 'yobbo' I've ever seen. But, in actual fact, he was the most feared hooligan of the Eighties. What's even more amazing is that over 2,000 West Ham supporters petitioned Downing Street for Cass's release from prison, after he was remanded for a crime he never committed.

When big Cass Pennant is on a mission, there is no stopping him. No wonder he commands such respect and has such a reputation and, boy, oh boy, can he have a 'row'!

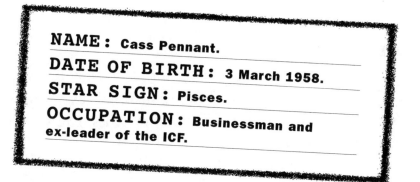

NAME: Cass Pennant.

DATE OF BIRTH: 3 March 1958.

STAR SIGN: Pisces.

OCCUPATION: Businessman and ex-leader of the ICF.

BACKGROUND

I was a Dr Barnado's kid and was brought up in a home in Barking. Eventually, I was fostered. I was lucky, I wasn't passed from family to family like an old parcel. The first family I was placed with I stayed with. They were a white couple who were very old and had old-fashioned values, principles and morals. They didn't have a lot of money but what they did have was love, and plenty of it. I was brought up in a town in Kent called Erith, which was an all-white area. I was the only black kid on the block; in fact, I was the only black kid in the town, so I was always picked on – a target.

It soon became apparent that the only way to escape my abusers was to stand up and fight. I fought tooth and nail, no matter what the size of the persecutor. By the time I was 11 years old, I already had a reputation for fighting and soon found that instead of wanting to bash me, my tormentors wanted to be my friend. I was accepted; one of the lads.

At times, it seemed I fought every day. If it wasn't in the street, then it was at football matches and, in particular, at West Ham.

LIFE OF CRIME

My first arrest was when I was 17 for possessing offensive weapons. I've been arrested for similar serious offences six times, all for violence at football matches. I've served four years in prison.

WEAPONRY

I like to use my fists.

TOUGHEST MOMENTS

I've had all sorts of experiences with a number of unsavoury characters. I've been run through with a sword and I've been shot at point-blank range. But the most frightening experience of my life was in a train after a football match.

It was a Saturday afternoon in 1981. West Ham had just played Sheffield Wednesday and won. Spirits were high and we were in a fighting mood. We walked through the streets chanting and singing, 'West Ham ... West Ham ...'

Word on the street was that there had been a fight in another part of town and a kid had been stabbed. For once, it was nothing to do with us.

We made our way to the station and boarded the fast train from Sheffield to London. Half-way back to London, the train was stopped and police swarmed on to the carriages. We were still singing and making a bit of a nuisance of ourselves. The police took statements from other passengers along the lines of, 'It's the black bloke. He's the ringleader.'

It was only then it became apparent that it was to do with the stabbing. The police were looking for the perpetrator – a white man with blond hair carrying a knife. They interviewed everybody on the train but for some strange reason I was singled out and arrested. I couldn't have looked any less like the person they were looking for if I tried. I was a 6ft black man with afro hair and I certainly wasn't carrying a knife. Under protest, I was taken to a police station and put in a cell.

Later, a few Old Bill came in. What I wasn't expecting was for them to say that I had to tell them who'd stabbed the kid. They also said that the kid was in a bad way and was unlikely to make it through the night.

Then I was charged with murder and was looking at life imprisonment. I felt powerless. That was the toughest moment in my life. I can fight a man holding a gun or a knife when I can see what I'm up against, but I can't fight the powers that be. I ain't no grass, never have been and never will be.

At that moment, I was prepared to do life if I had to. The police tried their hardest to convict me, but truth prevailed and I walked free from Snaresbrook Court, thank God.

IS THERE ANYONE YOU ADMIRE?

Frank Bruno. He was a man who came from nothing but he had a goal and he achieved it. He had people who knocked him all the way. He's been laughed at and told he can't box his way out of a paper bag. He came through all that with flying colours and, most of all, the British public love him, so he's the winner. Frank Bruno brings hope to every under-privileged street kid. It was his success that drove me on.

DO YOU BELIEVE IN HANGING?

No, I don't believe in hanging. We live in a civilised society where there are other forms of punishment for criminals but, for proven nonce cases where they cannot live in society, there is only one cure – death, by whatever form society deems suitable.

IS PRISON A DETERRENT?

No. In my experience it's a criminal college. A man will go in a burglar and come out a fraudster. A drug dealer goes in selling cannabis and soft drugs and comes out selling heroin.

WHAT WOULD HAVE DETERRED YOU FROM A LIFE OF CRIME?

Crime is nothing to do with parenting. It's down to the company you keep and the area in which you live. If someone lives on a run-down council estate in Glasgow where there are no jobs, no hope and no way out, then crime is the only alternative.

WHAT MAKES A TOUGH GUY?

When I saw my wife giving birth, it suddenly made me think and put it all into perspective. That here was someone tougher than anyone I'd ever met – my wife. That was on a personal level. In the big bad world of reality a real tough guy never considers himself to be tough. He's just himself.

CASS'S FINAL THOUGHT

I've been a bad lad and I've done some good in my life but I'm not ashamed of anything I've done or the choices I've made; like the decision to do life imprisonment rather than grass.

Most of the times I've been in trouble have been down to the colour of my skin, but I think racism is better today because in my day you would rarely see black girls with white blokes and vice versa.

Today, people don't bother so much, unless, of course, you're in prison. I suffered more from racial abuse inside than anywhere else. The white screws hated me because I was black. The blacks hated me because I spoke with a cockney accent; they thought I was trying to be a choc-ice. They didn't know that I was brought up by white parents and why should I tell them? Why should I tell anyone anything? Fuck 'em! It ain't nobody's business but my own.

HARD BASTARD

Steve Arneil

STEVE ARNEƒL

While researching this book, the name Steve Arneil kept cropping up. First from Cass Pennant, then from Stilks and finally from a couple of others. Every one of them said the same thing: 'You will never get Steve to agree to an interview.'

It was a few phone calls later that I managed to obtain Steve's telephone number. I wasn't sure how I was going to approach the subject of a book on hard bastards, but I'd heard so much about him that I thought, sod it, take the bull by the horns, so I telephoned him. To my surprise, he was very modest and from the moment I spoke to him he had a kind of aura, just through his voice. I explained what I was doing and he laughed, 'I'm not a hard man.'

I didn't want to let the opportunity pass and persuaded him to let me speak to him face to face. With a bit of a push and a pull he eventually agreed. Arrangements were made for me to go to Crystal Palace the following Thursday evening.

As I walked into the sports centre, the smell of cheesy feet on rubber mats was overwhelming. Some kids were playing basketball. The screeching sound of trainers on polished floorboards made me shudder. I asked a fit-looking youth where the karate class was being held. Cass interrupted; he was waiting for me, to introduce me to Steve.

From the moment I met Steve Arneil, he had an overriding inner peace about him. It sounds silly or maybe I've been watching too much TV, but I almost felt as if I had to bow. I've been told that he has that effect on other people and I'm not just being melodramatic.

Steve took me upstairs and we sat and talked. He told me that he'd trained with the monks in Japan and elsewhere in the Far East. Steve had an aura about him and I felt that he was a man with an inner calm and an inner strength. It is difficult for me to do justice in words to Steve's mannerisms, his gestures and the way that he tells a story. He's a bit of a mystery. I found him a unique man, an enigma. I don't know that much about him. He's not the sort of person that I usually deal with and he's unlike any other man in this book. He's a straight, law-abiding citizen. But ... I've no doubt that he is an incredibly dangerous man.

I've heard it said that your eyes are the windows to your soul. I looked deep into the eyes of the world karate champion, Steve Arneil, and he had an unmistakable look in his eyes, one that says, 'You fuck with me and I'll kill you,' but in a more restrained, subtle way than many other hard bastards.

NAME: Steve Arneil.

DATE OF BIRTH: 29 August 1934.

STAR SIGN: Virgo.

OCCUPATION: World Karate Champion.

BACKGROUND

I was born in South Africa. Then, when I was 12, my parents emigrated to Northern Rhodesia, now called Zambia.

I have always been a keen sportsman. I learned judo at a very young age, reaching my black belt in Tokyo, Japan, when I was 17. I also played rugby and managed to get to international status. I did boxing too, but my mother was in the medical profession and didn't like the way I kept being hit on the head.

Then one day I saw a Chinese gentleman in a small shop. He was doing strange moves, ones that I'd never seen before. I watched him for ages, mesmerised. Finally, he stopped and we started to talk. He explained that he was practising a Chinese form of karate called Shoring Tempo. From that day on, I decided that I wanted to go East. It's funny, because all my life I've been drawn to the East, so when I decided to travel there it seemed the most natural thing to do.

I managed to get a job on a boat as a mechanical

engineer and worked my way from South Africa to Japan. First I went to China and studied under the monks. Unfortunately due to political problems – Mao Tse Tung and his little red book – I had to get out of the country, and quick. My teachers in the temple said that they'd heard talk of a gentleman in Japan who'd be a suitable teacher. The man was called Mas Oyama.

I travelled to Japan in the hope of finding this man, which was difficult because I didn't speak Japanese.

By chance, I met an American called Don Drager, a writer who studies martial arts. I told him I was searching for Mas Omaya. He said he knew where he was; I couldn't believe my luck. He took me to meet Mas Omaya and after much talk he agreed for me to be his pupil.

I trained in Japan for five years. The five years of training was extraordinarily demanding. The particular form of karate is called Gouda – it's very hard, but Mas Omaya was the Master. He was the strongest man I'd ever met. He killed bulls with his bare hands and fought 200 men without stopping.

When he thought I was ready, he said he would arrange for me to fight 100 men. I thought he was crazy, but he was serious. I trained every day in the mountains or in the sea and on the beaches. I asked my master every day – when would I fight?

Then one Sunday I walked into the dojo to do my training. Everyone was waiting for me. Mas Omaya said, 'Today you fight 100 men.'

It took two-and-three-quarter hours.

LIFE OF CRIME

I've never had any involvement with the law. I've never been to prison or to court. I've always managed to talk myself out of situations.

WEAPONRY

I have very strong arms. I also have good legs.

TOUGHEST MOMENT

My 100-man fight. I've only done it once.

IS THERE ANYONE YOU ADMIRE?

My teacher Mas Omaya. He is known throughout the world. He guided me and taught me a lot about life – humility, respect, courtesy and also how to give other people enjoyment in their lives.

DO YOU BELIEVE IN HANGING?

Yes, I do believe in hanging, providing the society we live in is fair and honest. I think if someone has taken a life, in particular the life of a child, they have to pay for it.

IS PRISON A DETERRENT?

Some people go to prison and learn their lesson, while others come back ten times worse. Prison is meant as a punishment, not as a deterrent.

WHAT WOULD HAVE DETERRED YOU FROM A LIFE OF CRIME?

I'm clean.

WHAT MAKES A TOUGH GUY?

Courtesy and politeness is very important. Just because you're courteous doesn't mean you're weak. The character of a person can signify strength, it's not just physical ability. When I fought the 100 men, I was very strong and fit but I had mental strength to keep my line of direction and hold it.

STEVE'S FINAL THOUGHT

I don't consider myself a tough guy or a hard man. But only a fool takes my kindness as a weakness. I do not look for trouble and will avoid it wherever necessary, but if I was in a situation that meant protecting somebody I loved, I would have no hesitation in taking it all the way, and if that means to kill, then so be it.

HARD BASTARD

Stellakis
Stylianou

STELLAKIS STYLIANOU

Stilks' physique is that of an athlete, he's wiry and fast. In his line of work, speed is of the essence – and I don't mean a 'dab' of the white powder. He has to be able to defuse situations before they erupt into violence. The difference between him and most other meaty doormen is experience. I hate to quote a corny cliché, but he has been there, done it, and got every fucking T-shirt available.

I asked Stilks whether perhaps he thrived on dangerous situations and did he ever get nervous.

'Nah, I don't get nervous. I wasn't even worried when a gang was going to lynch me for refusing them entry to a club. It's just part and parcel of security work.'

I studied his rugged face. His strong features gave nothing away. He has a protruding nose and beady eyes and gives the impression that he is almost bombproof. I interviewed him at his home in Sidcup on the outskirts of London. As I knocked on the front door, I noticed that one of the windows was broken. Once inside, I asked his pretty wife Sheena how it was broken. She tutted and sighed, 'It's 'im. He forgot his keys again.'

She went on to tell me that Stilks is forgetful – 'It's his age,' she teased.

'I'm not old,' he winked. 'I can still chase you round the kitchen and catch ya!' They looked at each other and laughed, sharing a private joke.

They were obviously a couple who were comfortable with each other and still very much in love after 24 years of marriage. Stilks waited until his wife left the room, then whispered, 'She's pregnant again, ya know. I've got four daughters, maybe this time we'll have a boy, then I'll retire from working on the doors. But don't mention it to Sheena ... Shh, she's coming back ...'

Stilks was like a naughty boy. The cat that ate the cream. Sheena put the tea down on the polished coffee table and smiled a radiant smile. Stilk's puffed his chest out with pride. They were a smashing couple.

I was glad Stilks was considering retiring from door work. It was a nice thought and an even nicer thing to say to his pregnant wife. But I think the promise may have been made in haste, maybe in the flush of pride of an expectant father.

I really think the word retirement is not applicable to men like Stilks; it's more suited to bank managers and accountants. When you've been a tough guy all your life, you can't just give it up, it's not that simple, because you can never retire from what and who you really are...

NAME: Stellakis Stylianou.

DATE OF BIRTH: 21 July 1958.

STAR SIGN: I'm a Cancerian, born on the cusp, and I like to think I'm more of a Leo.

OCCUPATION: Professional doorman.

BACKGROUND

I was born in Plumstead, South London. Although I was born in England, I couldn't speak English until I was seven. My parents were from Cyprus. Mum and Dad tried to be strict with me, but by the age of 14 I'd become uncontrollable. Then I started going to a local youth club and was introduced to judo – I loved it. It was a way of expressing myself in a positive rather than negative way. It became a way of life and I enjoyed it for 12 years. Each level and each belt I won gave me great satisfaction and when I won my black belt by beating a line-up of six opponents one after the other, it was the pièce de résistance!

LIFE OF CRIME

Nothing to speak of.

WEAPONRY

I've hit a few people with chairs but I never carry a knife

or a knuckle-duster because I think, on the spur of the moment, I'd use it. I've broken my hand five times where I've hit people on the head. So I find the quickest and easiest way to control a violent situation is to use strangulation.

TOUGHEST MOMENT

It was late August and the football season had just started. I was working on a door at a hotel. Millwall supporters were celebrating a win. They were full of lager and up for a row. I was having none of it and told them to leave. There was a bit of a scuffle but I got them out and thought no more of it.

At the end of the night, as usual, I was hungry and fancied a kebab. I told the boys to start locking up and that I wouldn't be long. I made my way down a dimly lit road towards the late-night take-away. Call it a gut feeling or instinct, but I felt I was being followed. I couldn't quite put my finger on it, but something didn't feel right.

Half-way down the road I heard footsteps behind me. I glanced over my shoulder and saw four blokes running towards me with sticks. I recognised them as the men I'd thrown out of the club earlier.

In my panic, I looked around but there was no one in sight. I had no alternative but to run towards my attackers. I grabbed the stick off the first bloke and bashed him round the head with it and he fell to the floor. I thought, If I'm going to get done, I'm taking this one with me. I pushed my fingers into his eyes and he screamed in agony. The others started beating me over the head and back, but I didn't care. All I focused on was keeping a firm grip on the one I had on the floor. He was screaming like a stuffed pig.

In a situation like that you don't really feel pain, the adrenalin blocks it out. I was taking blows from every angle. I was hit on the left side of my head, then the right, I saw stars and for a moment I thought I was going to pass out. But I held on – I had to. I just remember car headlights, people screaming and noise – then nothing. I thought I was dead.

IS THERE ANYONE YOU ADMIRE?

A man called Johnny Madden. He was head doorman at the Camden Palace and also at the Hippodrome. Johnny Madden is a man of respect and a man of principle. He gently eased me into door work and told me the dos and don'ts. That was 23 years ago and we've remained friends ever since.

DO YOU BELIEVE IN HANGING?

Yes. For paedophiles and serial rapists. Not forgetting the serial killers. String 'em up! That's all they deserve.

IS PRISON A DETERRENT?

Yes, for some. On one hand I've got a friend, a good friend who's a big, strong and well-respected man. I worked with him on the doors for ten years. He was a brave, fearless man, who wasn't frightened to take risks. He was sentenced to nine months in prison and he did six, but he couldn't muck it. When he came out of prison, he didn't leave his house for a year. I've asked him many times to come back on the door, but he refuses. He got himself a little 9 – 5 job and became 'normal'. So, yes, it deterred him.

On the other hand, I've got friends who've done five, ten, fifteen years and they're still active. It didn't deter them. So it depends on the make-up of the individual.

WHAT WOULD HAVE DETERRED YOU FROM A LIFE OF CRIME?

If I thought that I would not be able to see my wife and kids for a long period of time, then that would deter me. In saying that, when you're up to no good, you don't think you're going to get caught.

WHAT MAKES A TOUGH GUY?

If I hit a man and knock him down and he jumps to his feet and comes back at me, then I knock him down for the second time and he still won't give in – is he a hard bastard or a stupid one? In my eyes, he has no fear, which makes him a tough guy.

STILKS' FINAL THOUGHT

I've done door work for 23 years and in that time I've had to deal with many confrontations in which I've felt my life was being threatened. I've been attacked by people you'd never dream in a million years would attack you. When I was first on the door I was gullible and I'd give people the benefit of the doubt.

On a cold Saturday night I stood on the door with my hands deep in my overcoat pockets. A customer tried to get into the club and I noticed he was wearing jeans, so I refused him entry.

'Is it all right if I wait here?' he asked, shivering in the doorway.

I shrugged. 'If you like.'

For the next ten minutes I saw people in and out of the club. Suddenly with no warning, the man standing in the doorway hit me over the back of the head and ran up the road.

I was stunned. For a moment I leaned against the wall to gather my thoughts. This was lesson number one: when you tell someone to go, they go. There are no exceptions.

I hold the dubious record for being the longest-serving doorman. During my time as a doorman I've been hit, punched and shot at. The lesson I learned is: never underestimate anyone, no matter how big or small.

HARD BASTARD

Johnny Frankham

JOHNNY FRANKHAM

'Whatever you do, don't mention his ear!'

I looked at Johnny Frankham; he looked at me; his face was dead-pan. As we approached his brother Sam, I noticed that half his ear was missing. There was a group of travelling boys all around us. Again, he whispered, 'Whatever you do, don't mention his ear.'

Sam approached me with an outstretched hand. I shook his hand and smiled. Automatically, my eyes were drawn to his ear – if you can call it an ear. It looked more like a pig's corkscrew tail.

'There,' Johnny said, 'you looked at it ... you looked at his ear, didn't you?'

I wasn't sure if he was joking or serious.

I smirked. 'I didn't, I didn't look.'

Johnny's face gave nothing away, he was adamant. 'Yes, you did. You looked at his ear, I saw you, and so did

Sam.'

For a moment there was a silence. All the travelling boys looked at me; I looked at Johnny, his rugged face expressionless. Phil – the man who'd brought me to the campsite and was responsible for my safety – stood nearby. I glanced at him for something, I don't really know what, reassurance maybe. Phil winked. Only then I knew that Johnny was pulling my leg. The gypsy boys erupted into coarse, raucous laughter and I heaved a sigh of relief.

I'd gone to Berkshire to meet Johnny Frankham and his brother Sammy, King of the Gypsies. I wasn't really sure what to expect. We all have preconceived ideas of what gypsies look and live like and I was expecting to see grubby-looking men standing around bonfires with wild, untamed horses tied to a stake in a muddy field. There would probably be small children with dirty faces and snotty noses, running around swearing and spitting.

As we approached the campsite, it was snowing; a thick layer of snow covered the trailers. Nobody was around, just a skinny dog tied to a kennel on a long piece of threadbare rope, barking his head off.

Phil climbed out of his Mercedes and called out to a dark-skinned lady standing in her doorway,

'Where's Johnny at?'

She pointed. 'Down the end, last trailer on the right.'

I looked around; brand-new Mercedes cars were parked outside spanking new mobile homes. Each was surrounded by white picket fences and neatly kept gardens. I was shocked – it was not at all what I had expected. I was apprehensive; after all, we were strangers to the campsite. Everyone wanted to know who we were and, more importantly, what we were doing there. Net curtains twitched; suspicion filled the air as we crunched our way through the snow towards the end trailer.

Waiting for us was a tall, good-looking man, immaculately dressed. Phil made the introduction, 'This is Johnny Frankham.'

'Come in,' he said.

I walked into Johnny Frankham's home. I bent to take my shoes off, but Johnny shook his head. I stepped into the kitchen and the smell of Sunday roast was delicious. A small, pretty lady wearing a pinnie and big gold earrings smiled.

'Cup of tea, luv?' she asked.

Her kitchen cabinets were full to bursting with Crown Derby china. She handed me a bone china cup and saucer full of steaming hot tea which I drank with caution. I wasn't used to drinking tea from such fine china.

I was shown into the lounge and stepped on to white, thick pile carpet which wouldn't have looked out of place at the Dorchester. The room was magnificent; all white curtains with swags and tails, embroidered with gold sashes, white leather sofas and gold-edged mirrors.

Before Johnny agreed to be in the book, I had to explain in detail exactly what the book was about. After much careful thought on his part, and a little gentle persuasion on mine, he gave in.

We left the others sitting in the lounge, went into the dining room and sat at a beautiful table with a huge bowl of fresh fruit set in the middle of it.

I turned on my tape recorder and Johnny started to talk. He was a very quiet, unassuming man, not boastful in the slightest. In fact, I found him to be extremely modest, but there was something in his eyes – just something.

After the interview, he took me by the hand and showed me into a small room where his grandchildren were playing. On the wall were photographs of Johnny at the height of his boxing career. There was one photograph that caught my eye, in which Johnny stood over a man lying on the canvas. I asked him about it. He laughed.

'That's Muhammad Ali. I used to be his sparring partner when he was known as Cassius Clay.'

I was shocked – Muhammad Ali! Was this just another one of his wind-ups? But it was no joke. I read through the newspaper cuttings shaking my head in disbelief, but there it was in black and white – Cassius Clay lying on the floor in front of Johnny Frankham. It was unbelievable, there I was in a trailer in the middle of the Berkshire countryside with the man who'd knocked the greatest boxer that had ever lived to the ground. No wonder Johnny Frankham has such a fearsome reputation.

But Johnny being Johnny, he just shrugged. He wouldn't say whether it was a lucky punch, whether he hit him or whether he didn't. He just left it to my own speculation.

'Come on,' he said. 'Come and meet my brother Sam – but whatever you do, don't mention his ear …'

NAME: Johnny Frankham.
DATE OF BIRTH: 6 June 1948.
STAR SIGN: Gemini.
OCCUPATION: King of the Gypsies.

BACKGROUND

I was born in a tent in a field. My family have travelled all over the country. I don't come from a big family. I've got two brothers and a sister. From the age of six we toured gypsy camps going hop or fruit picking, depending on the season. It's natural for travelling boys to fight, but when we were kids it was never done for money. As you grow up as a gypsy, things change and it becomes more competitive.

I started amateur boxing when I was 14. I went through my amateur career and won all the ABAs. In between, I'd have fights with other travellers and various others who wanted to have a go. I met some tough ones, too. My brother Sam and I were the first travelling boys to start proper training and go legit. People thought we were a push-over. But me and Sam would always end up thrashing our opponents. I've got to say, I enjoyed boxing. I wasn't bad at it either.

LIFE OF CRIME

I've been in every prison in the country, but I'd rather not say why.

WEAPONRY

I've always fought with my fists, but I've kicked a few people and nutted a few people. It's part of the game.

TOUGHEST MOMENT

It was tough when I fought my brother Sam because we were friends as well as brothers. We fell out loads of times but the first time I had to fight him was hard. He's a tough man, but at the time I was more educated than him and I'd done more training, so I beat him.

IS THERE ANYONE YOU ADMIRE?

I admire any man who'll stand up and have a fight and won't back down.

DO YOU BELIEVE IN HANGING?

Yes, for paedophiles and perverts.

IS PRISON A DETERRENT?

No. Prison is a stepping stone for people who want to commit crime. They learn more about crime and drugs in prison than they do outside.

WHAT WOULD HAVE DETERRED YOU FROM A LIFE OF CRIME?

Money is the only thing that would have deterred me. Crime is all down to money. All the times I've been in trouble were down to a pound note.

WHAT MAKES A TOUGH GUY?

The way you are brought up affects the way you are. If you're brought up tough then you're bound to be tough. You can't take someone out of an office and make him tough. It's all down to upbringing.

I'd rather fight someone that I knew could have a fight than someone who's a coward. You haven't got to be afraid of a man who'll fight you, but the man that's afraid could shoot you.

JOHNNY'S FINAL THOUGHT

I've had fights all over the place – fairgrounds, racetracks, fields and clubs. I know from experience that if there's a gang, it's going to be a hard fight. A man will keep fighting in front of his mates until he drops. I've banged heads, I've punched them, I've kicked them and they've still got up just because the crowd's egging them on. When the crowd's not there they just take the beating. I've been stabbed and I've been shot, but I have no regrets. Whatever I've done to another man, I've done because he deserved it.

HARD BASTARD

ALBERT READING

ALBERT READING

Look up the word 'gangster' and the definition will read 'Albert Reading'. Albert is a mine of information and knows everyone there is to know, from as far away as Scotland and Liverpool. If you want anything, need anything or even need to speak to anyone, then Albert's your man.

He's infamously known as 'Boom Boom Reading.' I asked him how he got his nickname. Was it because he was known to use both gun barrels? Or was it because he was formerly a bare-knuckle fighter with punches like bombs? Albert threw his head back and laughed noisily. It wasn't any of those things. He's known as Boom Boom because he's as sly as a fox, and the puppet Basil Brush was a fox whose catch-phrase was 'boom boom'.

Unlike most gangsters, Albert Reading has got a sense of humour. Maybe it's because he's a Gemini and all

Geminis have a split personality. In ancient days, Gemini was symbolised by twin children – Castor and Pollux of Roman mythology. Split personality is a typical Gemini trait and Albert is a typical Gemini.

On one side of the coin he is nice, good with people and sociable, the life and soul of the party, a perfect host. On the other, he's ruthless, unpredictable and can be 'fucking 'orrible' when he wants! He's a dinosaur, an old-fashioned gangster with old-fashioned ways and morals. A dying breed.

In the year 2000, Albert will have turned 68 years old, but to him age is just a number. It hasn't slowed him down in any way, shape or form. Recently, he was given a Motability car to help him to get around. Just a normal, run-of-the-mill thing. Hundreds of people, for whatever reason, are given Motability cars and to the majority it is a big help. But Albert being Albert loaned his car to a friend – a friend who did an armed robbery in it. A Motability car on an armed robbery – some fucking friend!

'Fucking liberty,' Albert hissed. 'It was a mug-off collecting my Motability car from the police pound and even more of a mug-off that Motability took the car back!'

To Albert, the Motability saga was just an inconvenience. To him, it was nothing out of the ordinary, he took it all in his stride. How the fuck can anyone lose a Motability car in an armed robbery? It could only happen to Albert Reading.

NAME: Albert Reading.
DATE OF BIRTH: 6 June 1932.
STAR SIGN: Gemini.
OCCUPATION: Gangster.

BACKGROUND

I was born in West Ham, London, one of eight children. My father Joe was the lightweight boxer who fought under his mother's maiden name of Riley. He had over 200 fights in his long boxing career. Unfortunately, he never kept his punches in the boxing ring and he beat me like a man throughout my young life. I've got three other brothers: Charlie, Joey and, in particular, Bobby, who became a well-respected and feared man, owing to our father's misguided belief that if he treated them rough, they'd grow up tough.

LIFE OF CRIME

My first taste of prison was in 1944; my crime was stealing a bucket of potatoes. When my father was informed, he washed his hands of me and told the authorities to let me rot and teach the little bastard a lesson. I was taken to Standard House remand home in South London. I hated the home and two weeks later I beat the night watchman with a billiard cue and escaped.

When I was captured, I was sent to Wormwood Scrubs,

which was one of the toughest prisons in the country. I was 12 years old, the youngest person ever to be sent to the Scrubs.

Inside, I soon learned the jargon and the pecking order and, more importantly, who the 'Daddies' were. It seemed every inmate wanted a bit of me. If they didn't want to take my belongings, they wanted to take my body. I fought tooth and nail just to survive. Constantly in trouble, I was birched three times across the arse and was unable to sit down for a week.

I served six years for stealing a bucket of potatoes. When I was released back into the unsuspecting society at the age of 18, I was full of hate and anger. Unable to channel my aggression, I became as tough and as fearless as a wild animal, ready to wreak havoc on those who stood in my way.

For the next eight years, I stamped my mark on the underworld. Then in 1958, I committed my first armed robbery. I'd become uncontrollable, a maniac, public enemy number one and was hunted by police all over the country. My robberies became more and more violent.

By 1960, Scotland Yard caught me and I was sentenced to 25 years in prison. In all, I've spent more than three decades behind bars.

WEAPONRY

I'm known to use my fists or anything to hand – a piece of wood or iron bar – but I prefer to inflict the most excruciating pain by burning my victims with acid, literally, to melt their flesh. Nothing is taboo in my eyes, but I'm not into cutting. Violence works both ways.

I've been beaten half to death by a gang, almost cut in half by another and shot in the leg and shoulder. My whole life has been a catalogue of violent incidents, but I have no qualms or regrets about the pain I've dealt out or received. To me it's just swings and roundabouts.

TOUGHEST MOMENT

I've stood toe to toe with the élite of the underworld; I've fought and beat tough men like Charlie Richardson and Mad Frankie Fraser, but one of the toughest men I ever fought was the legendary Brian Hall, formerly Henry Cooper's sparring partner and some would say the greatest bare-knuckle fighter ever.

I stepped into the ring with Hall at the age of 48, Two rounds went my way; I broke Hall's nose and ribs, but in the third round Hall came back and beat me to the ground with cool, controlled ferocity, but still I wouldn't give in. Eventually, my corner dragged me out of the ring to save my life. The fight was one of the bloodiest this century.

IS THERE ANYONE YOU ADMIRE?

My sister Joanie, who died of a terminal illness. Just a few weeks before she died, I held her in my arms and she cried. She said she was frightened of dying. It broke my heart; I had no words of comfort. Nothing. I felt so helpless all I could do was hold her. She was so brave, the bravest person I've ever met.

DO YOU BELIEVE IN HANGING?

No. I was inside when hanging was still legal. I saw innocent men go to the gallows – a man called Hanratty and another, Flossy Forsyth.

IS PRISON A DETERRENT?

No. Prison makes you harder, shrewder and more cunning.

WHAT WOULD HAVE DETERRED YOU FROM A LIFE OF CRIME?

The war. If there hadn't been any blackouts, then I wouldn't have started robbing.

WHAT MAKES A TOUGH GUY?

Heart. I've seen hard men hit someone, but if they don't go over with the first punch then their heart goes.

ALBERT'S FINAL THOUGHT

I always wanted to be a gangster. When I was ten years old I nicked my dad's clothing coupons and exchanged them on the black market for a white pin-striped suit and a slug gun, just in case of trouble. It must have been an omen. When the suit fitted me that day, I knew I'd be the gangster I'd only ever dreamed of being.

All my life I've had to fight from backbone to breakfast time. It's been second nature. I don't know any different. I put that down to my father; he beat me mercilessly and turned me into a man when I was only a boy. The one thing he taught me, which I'm thankful for, was respect. It's a sad world when old ladies are mugged and children are abducted by paedophiles and abused. Cowards and bullies, that's all they are, preying on the old and vulnerable. Liberty-takers. I'll kill any man who tries to take a liberty with me or my family. That's not me being flash or talking big. Talk's cheap. I believe right is might.

The Bible reads: 'An eye for an eye, a tooth for a tooth.' Take a liberty with me and I'll rip both your eyes out and all your teeth. I'll beat you with my fist and an iron bar, burn you with acid or shoot you down like a dog because I can be wicked, but only if I have to be.

CONCLUSION

Now you've read the book and have had a rare opportunity to take a peek through the window into the lives of two dozen hard bastards, I think you'll agree that the hand-picked men featured are all top-of-the-tree tough guys – no question.

I wanted to write the book not because I'm a sticky beak or a nose ointment, but above all I thirst for knowledge and wanted to see if there were any similarities running through all of these men, any threads that linked them in any way.

Each and every one met the criteria of the three Rs – Respect, Reputation and can have a Row. But what else did they have in common? Undoubtedly, they all have an inbred sense of pride and honour. They would rather kill or be killed than let anyone take a liberty with them, that's for sure.

Some use violence to get money, and for others it's a grudge or perhaps pure survival. For the likes of Johnny Adair, the political animal, it's a burning passion for freedom in his country.

Many of them spoke fondly of the 'old school', and honour amongst thieves. So what really is the 'old school'? Certainly, I found the older men to have manners that men of today rarely possess. They know how to treat a lady. They would open doors and step back to let me through, take my coat for me, and watch their Ps and Qs, because it's not tough or clever to be uncouth. I found it a breath of fresh air to be around the older men. Perhaps that's what they mean by 'old school'?

But I didn't want only to interview men of the past but also of the future. I wanted to represent Britain as it is today in the year 2000. Britain has changed; society has changed; technology has taken over. The Victorian days have gone and with it went our pompous and arrogant ways. Some would say we threw the baby out with the bath water, but I disagree.

Britain has changed for the better. We are still regarded as Great Britain and should pride ourselves on our National Health Service and social security. There are people in the world who are starving, and if they're sick, they die. But not in Britain.

That's why so many people want to come here. We are a multi-cultural nation. A melting pot of black people, white people and coffee-coloured people. That's why I wanted to include people from different cultures.

Wherever I interviewed the contributors, be it Brixton,

Northern Ireland or just plain old Peckham High Street, I was treated the same – with politeness and respect. It proved to me that no matter where you come from, what religion or colour, we are all tribal and want to belong to ... to ... something. There are gypsies, Hell's Angels, skinheads, Catholics and Protestants; there are blacks and whites. But the one thing that is universal is that there are tough guys right across the board.

I like to think that *Hard Bastards* in its own way represents many of these sects. In a small way, I hope I've broken down the barriers and crossed boundaries. Tip-toed across them all. Each and every one of the tough guys I interviewed answered my questions truthfully and openly and amazingly agreed on many things:

100 per cent of the hard bastards agreed that age was a deciding factor as to whether prison is a deterrent.

100 per cent of the hard bastards agreed that paedophiles and rapists should hang.

50 per cent of the hard bastards were badly treated as children.

95 per cent of the hard bastards said money was the only thing that would have deterred them from a life of crime.

100 per cent of the hard bastards are against drugs.

100 per cent of the hard bastards are men of their word.

66 per cent of the hard bastards are heavily into physical training.

95 per cent of the hard bastards are totally paranoid.

95 per cent of the hard bastards have a sprinkling of madness.

But the one thing they all have in common is that they are all a bit tasty when it comes to 'avin' a tear-up. None of the men interviewed have been forced into their occupation, they have all chosen the business they are in – the business of violence.

After speaking with these men and listening to what they had to say I was surprised to find that 100 per cent of them, every single one, does not advocate violence and thinks that prison is a complete and utter waste of human life.

My only possible conclusion is that for some men – certainly for the two dozen hard bastards featured, they are not satisfied with the natural animal instinct to rip and tear – it's their inborn power and desire to chase, hunt and kill.

Also by Kate Kray

MURDER, MADNESS AND MARRIAGE
The love story of Britain's legendary gangster and his beautiful wife.

Price £4.99

NATURAL BORN KILLERS
Britain's eight deadliest murderers tell their own true stories.

Price £4.99

RONNIE KRAY: SORTED
The deathbed secrets of Britain's deadliest gangster.

Price £5.99

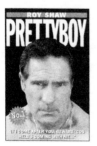

PRETTY BOY by Roy Shaw
The bestselling autobiography of one of the hardest bastards there is.

Price £14.99

Send off the coupon with cheque or credit card details to:
Blake Publishing Ltd., 3 Bramber Court, 2 Bramber Road,
London W14 9PB for your own copy.

I would like to order . . . . *Murder, Madness and Marriage* at £4.99 each
incl. p and p. and/or . . . . *Natural Born Killers* at £4.99 each
incl. p. and p. and /or . . . . *Ronnie Kray: Sorted* at £5.99 each
incl. p. and p. and /or . . . . *Pretty Boy* at £14.99 each

EITHER:
a. Debit my Visa/Access/Mastercard (delete as appropriate)
Card No . . . .
Expiry date . . . ./. . . . .
b. I enclose a cheque for . . . . made payable to Blake Publishing Ltd.
Name . . . .
Address . . . .
. . . .
. . . .
. . . .
Daytime telephone . . . .

(Please allow 28 days for delivery)